TEACH YOURSELF TO PLAY
GUITAR
Electric Guitar Songbook

ISBN 978-1-4234-1022-5

HAL•LEONARD®
CORPORATION
7777 W. BLUEMOUND RD. P.O. BOX 13819 MILWAUKEE, WI 53213

Visit Hal Leonard Online at
www.halleonard.com

CONTENTS

CD TRACK

		Demo	Play Along

		Demo	Play Along
4	**All the Small Things** **BLINK-182**	1	2
10	**Fun, Fun, Fun** **THE BEACH BOYS**	3	4
17	**A Hard Day's Night** **THE BEATLES**	5	6
22	**Smells Like Teen Spirit** **NIRVANA**	7	8
30	**Summer of '69** **BRYAN ADAMS**	9	10
38	**Sweet Home Chicago** **ROBERT JOHNSON**	11	12
44	**What I Like About You** **THE ROMANTICS**	13	14
49	**Wonderful Tonight** **ERIC CLAPTON**	15	16
54	**Guitar Notation Legend**		
	Tuning Notes	17	

All the Small Things

Words and Music by Tom De Longe and Mark Hoppus

Intro
Moderately fast Rock ♩ = 148

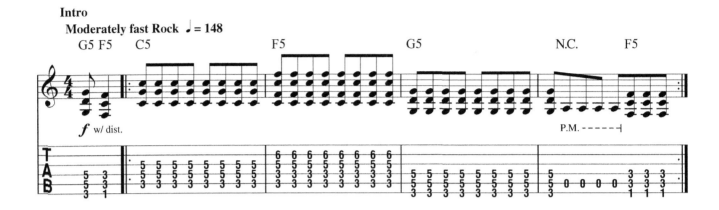

Verse

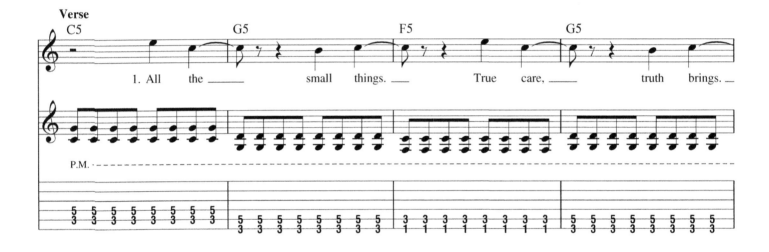

1. All the _____ small things. _____ True care, _____ truth brings. _____

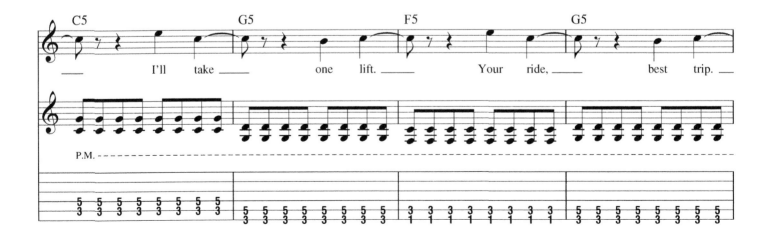

_____ I'll take _____ one lift. _____ Your ride, _____ best trip. _____

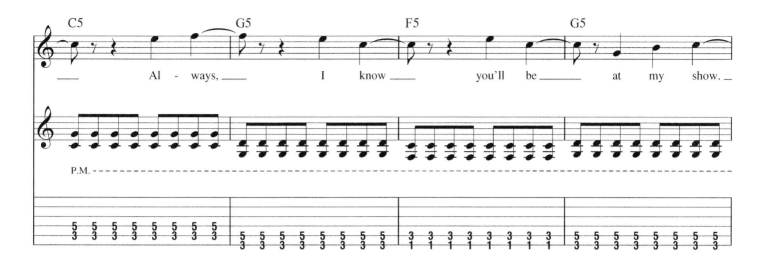

Al - ways, _____ I know ____ you'll be _____ at my show. __

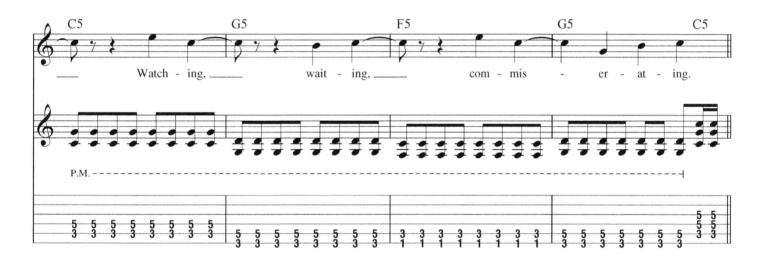

__ Watch - ing, _____ wait - ing, _____ com - mis - er - at - ing.

$\mathcal{S}$ Pre-Chorus

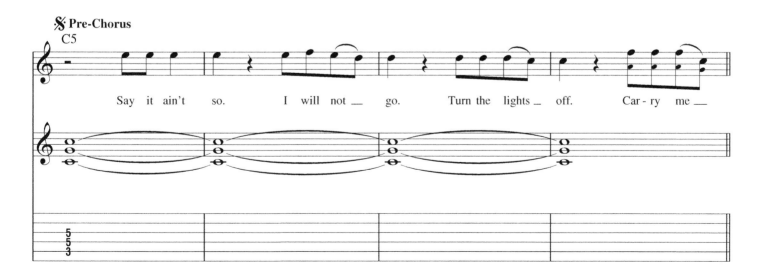

Say it ain't so. I will not __ go. Turn the lights __ off. Car - ry me __

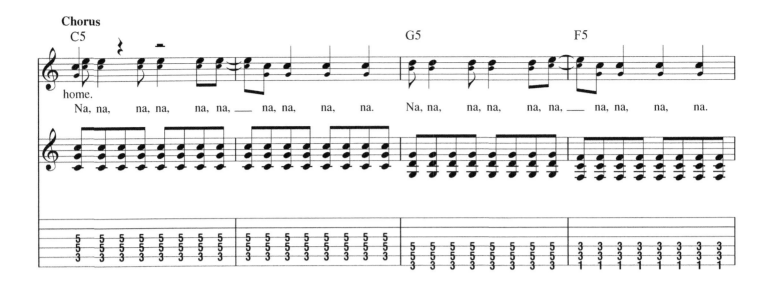

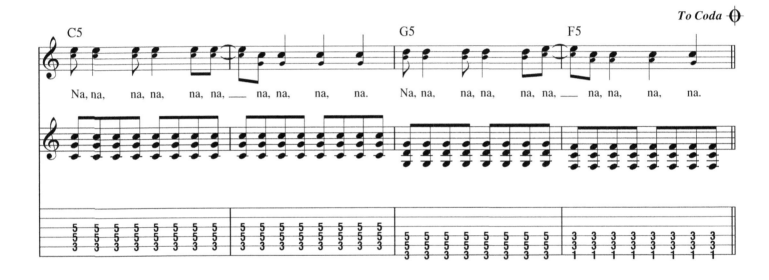

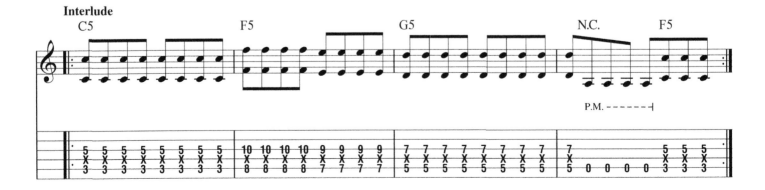

Verse

2. Late night, come home. ___ Work sucks, I know. _

D.S. al Coda

___ She left me ros - es by the stairs. _ Sur - pris-es let me know she cares. _

Coda

Interlude

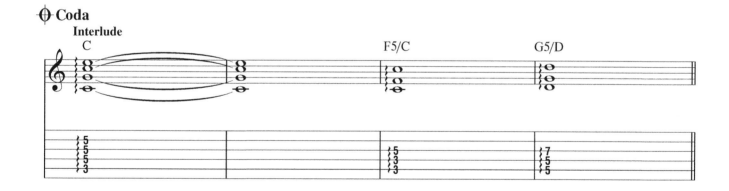

Play 3 times

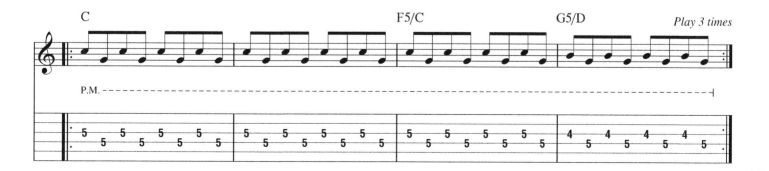

Say it ain't so. I will not __ go. Turn the lights __

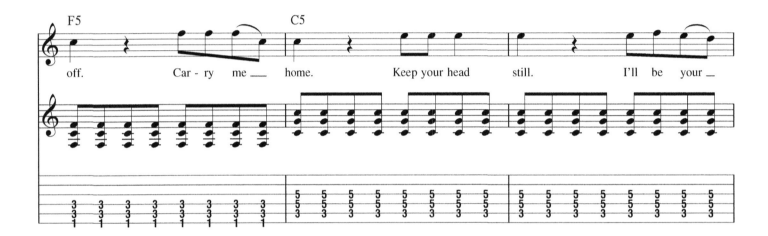

off. Car - ry me __ home. Keep your head still. I'll be your __

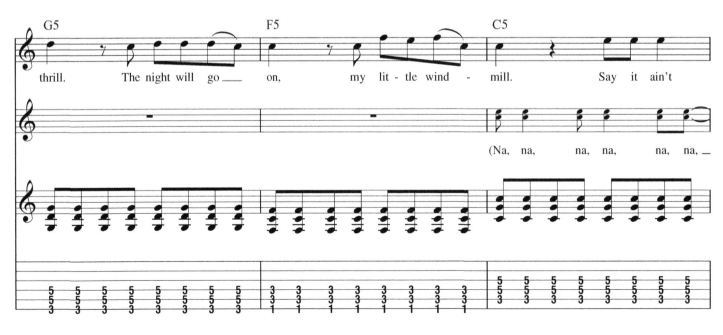

thrill. The night will go __ on, my lit - tle wind - mill. Say it ain't

(Na, na, na, na, na, na, __

so. I will not __ go. Turn the lights __ off. Car - ry me __

__ na, na, na, na. Na, na, na, na, na, na, __ na, na, na, na.

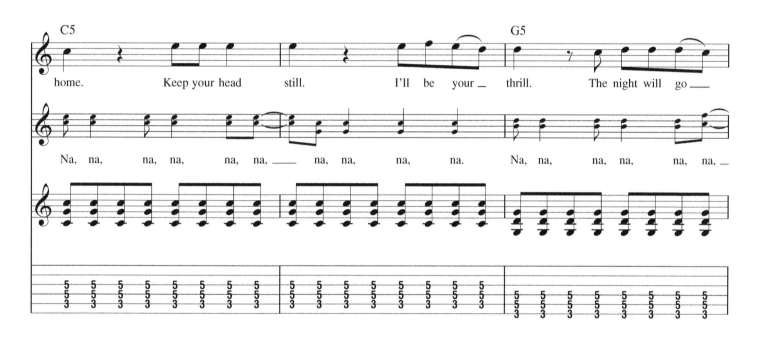

home. Keep your head still. I'll be your __ thrill. The night will go __

Na, na, na, na, na, na, __ na, na, na, na. Na, na, na, na, na, na, __

on, the night will go __ on, my lit - tle wind - mill.

__ na, na, na, na, na, __ na, na, na, na.)

Fun, Fun, Fun

Words and Music by Brian Wilson and Mike Love

Tune down 1/2 step:
(low to high) Eb-Ab-Db-Gb-Bb-Eb

Intro

Moderately fast ♩ = 168

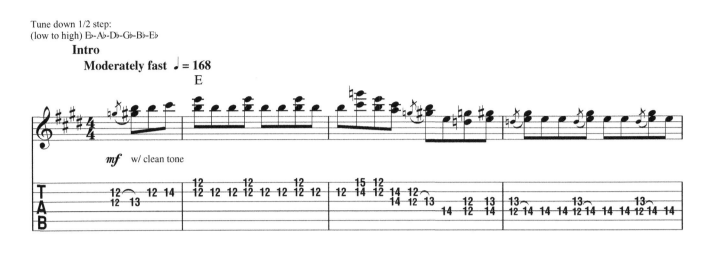

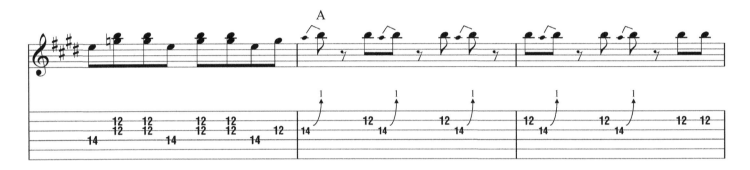

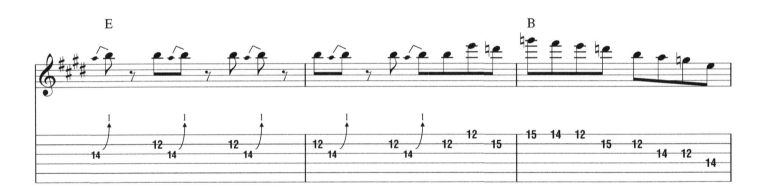

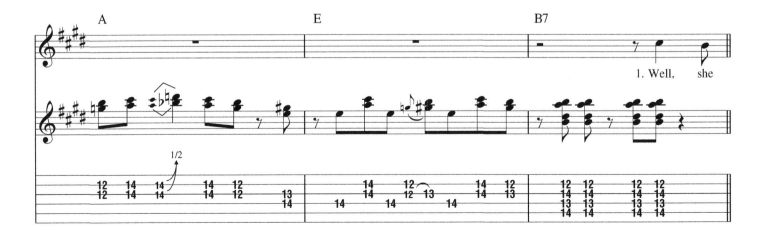

1. Well, she

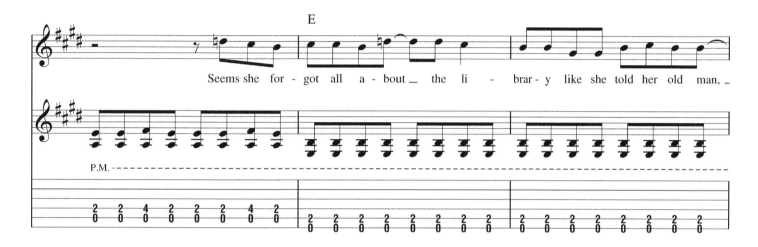

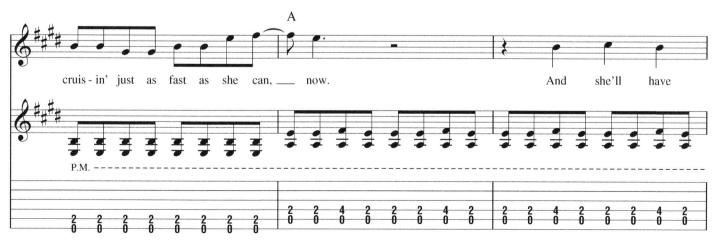

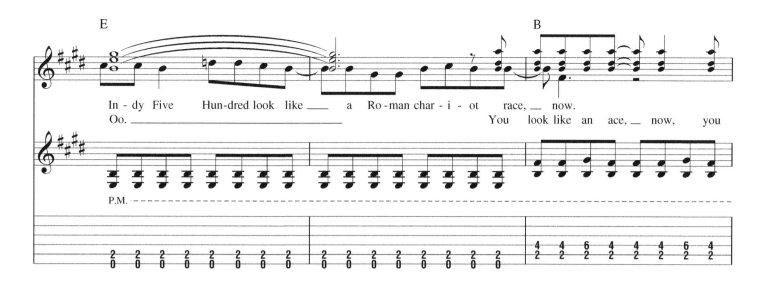

In - dy Five Hun-dred look like ___ a Ro - man char - i - ot race, ___ now.
Oo. _____ You look like an ace, ___ now, you

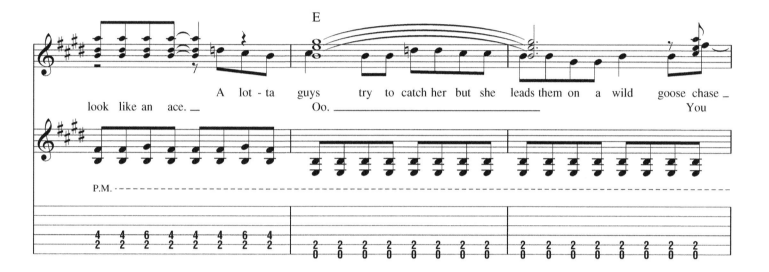

A lot - ta guys try to catch her but she leads them on a wild goose chase ___
look like an ace. ___ Oo. _____ You

___ now. And she'll have fun, fun, fun till her
drive like an ace, ___ now, you drive like an ace. ___ (Fun, fun, fun till her

Fun, fun, fun till her

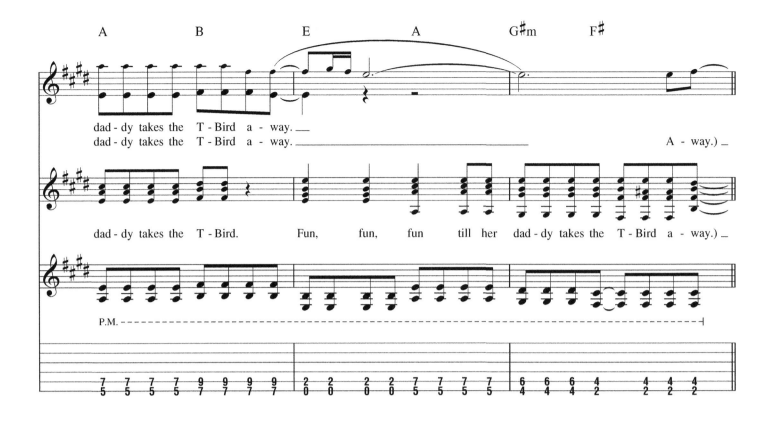

dad - dy takes the T - Bird a - way. ___
dad - dy takes the T - Bird a - way. _____
A - way.) _

dad - dy takes the T - Bird.   Fun,   fun,   fun   till her   dad - dy takes the T - Bird a - way.) _

P.M. --

Guitar Solo

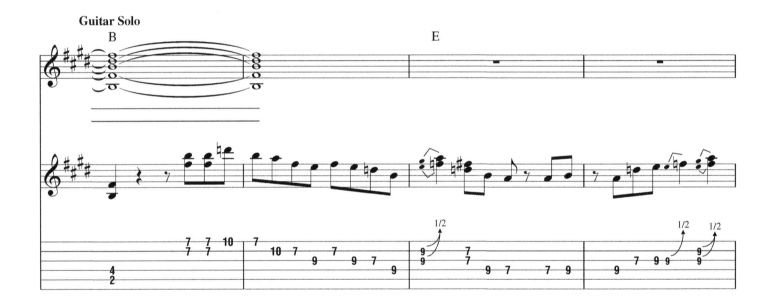

D.S. al Coda

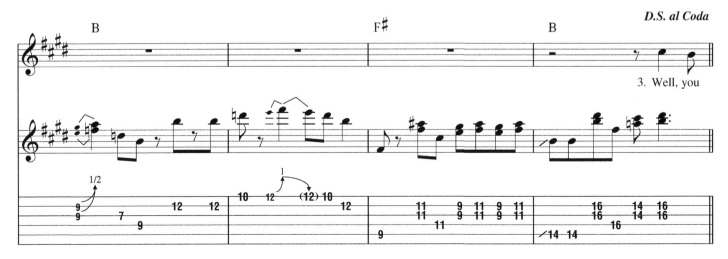

3. Well, you

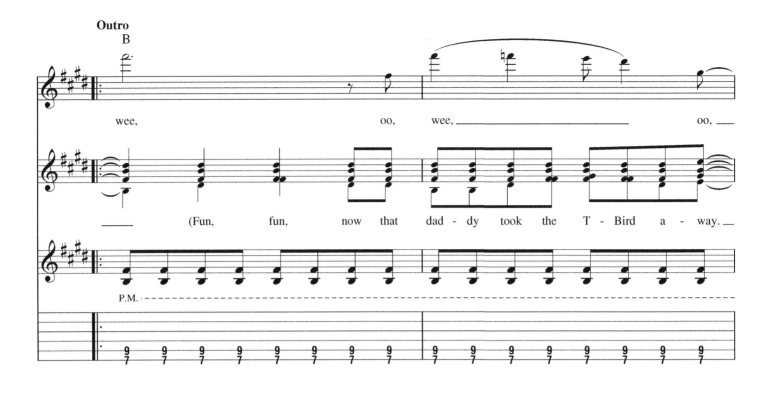

Outro

B

wee,   oo,   wee, _____   oo, ___

____ (Fun,   fun,   now   that   dad - dy   took   the   T - Bird   a - way. __

P.M. --

Repeat and fade

E

A

____   ah. _____   Oo,

____   Fun,   fun   now   that   dad - dy   took   the   T - Bird   a - way.) ___

P.M. --

Additional Lyrics

3. Well, you knew all along
   That your dad was gettin' wise to you, now.
   (You shouldn't have lied, now, you shouldn't have lied.)
   And since he took your set of keys
   You've been thinkin' that your fun is all through, now.
   (You shouldn't have lied, now, you shouldn't have lied.)
   But you can come along with me
   'Cause we got a lotta things to do now.
   (You shouldn't have lied, now, you shouldn't have lied.)
   And we'll..

A Hard Day's Night

Words and Music by John Lennon and Paul McCartney

Chorus

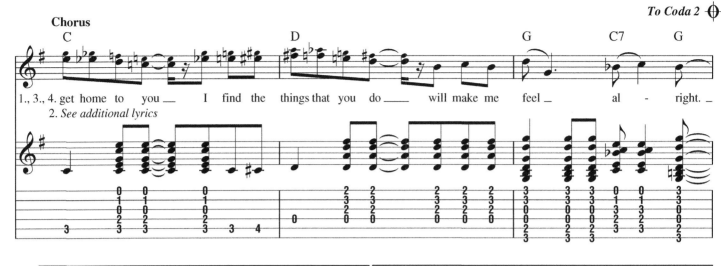

1., 3., 4. get home to you __ I find the things that you do __ will make me feel __ al - right. __
2. *See additional lyrics*

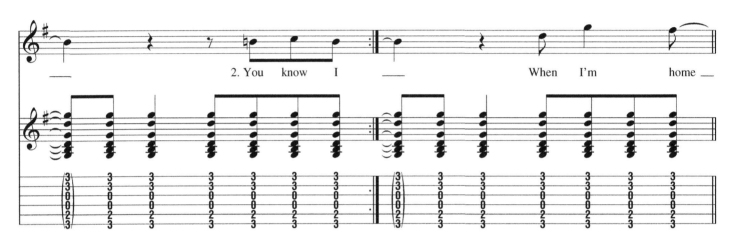

2. You know I __ When I'm home __

Bridge

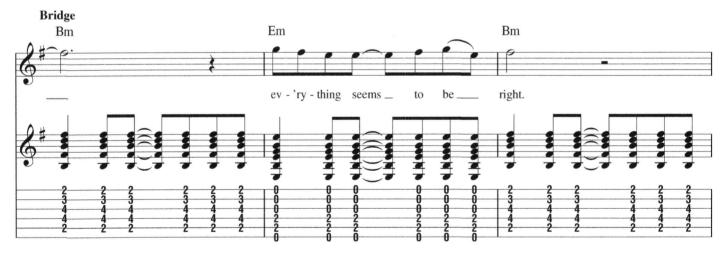

__ ev - 'ry - thing seems __ to be __ right.

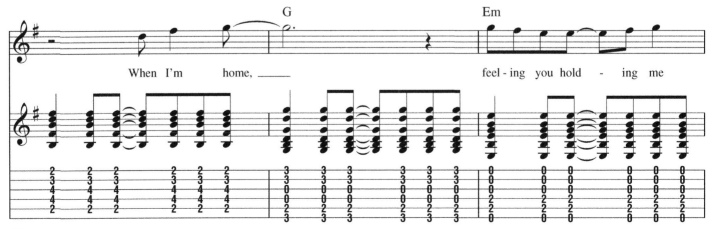

When I'm home, _____ feel - ing you hold - ing me

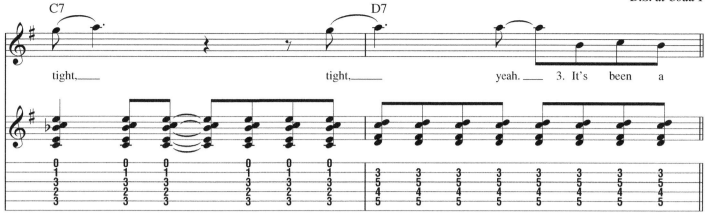

Coda 1

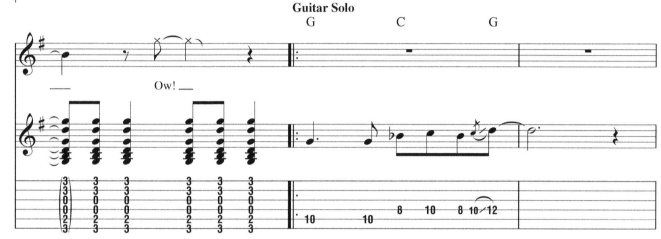

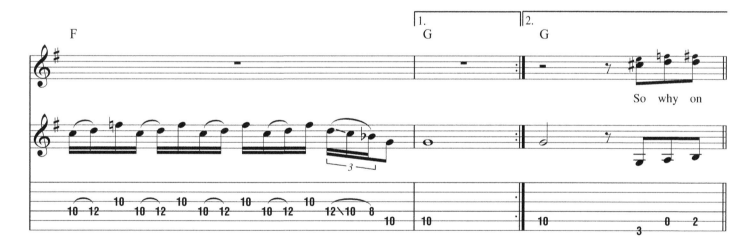

Chorus

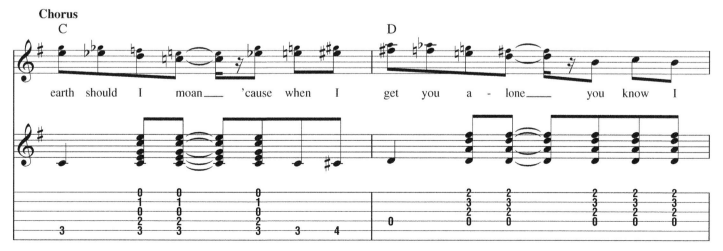

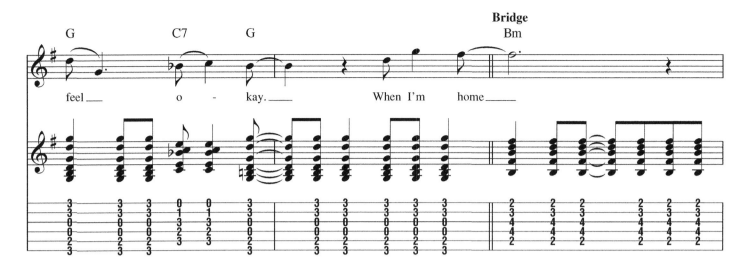

Bridge

G   C7   G   Bm

feel ___ o - kay. ___ When I'm home ___

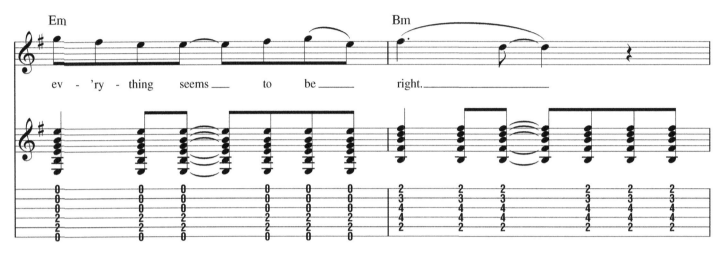

Em   Bm

ev - 'ry - thing seems ___ to be ___ right. ___

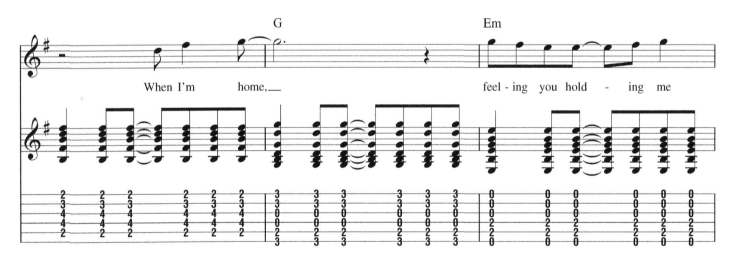

G   Em

When I'm home, ___ feel - ing you hold - ing me

D.S. al Coda 2

C7   D7

tight, ___ tight, ___ yeah. ___ 4. It's been a

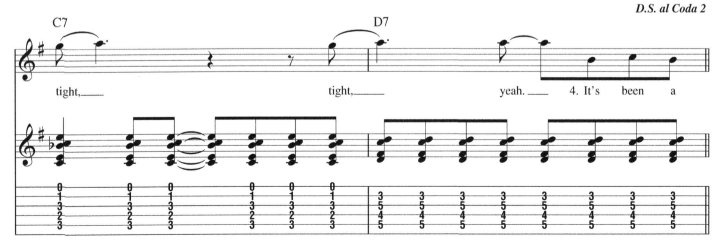

⊕ Coda 2

Outro

You know I feel ____ al - right. ____

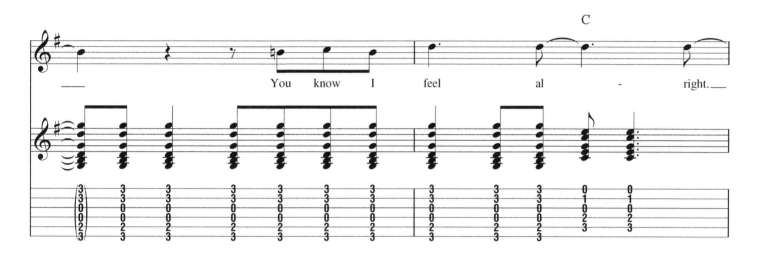

You know I feel al - right. ____

Repeat and fade

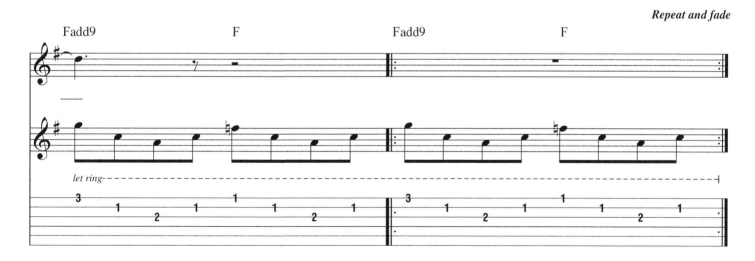

Additional Lyrics

2. You know I work all day,
  To get you money to buy your things.
  And it's worth it just to hear you say
  You're gonna give me ev'rything.

Chorus 2. So why on earth should I moan
  'Cause when I get you alone
  You know I feel okay.

Smells Like Teen Spirit

Words and Music by Kurt Cobain, Krist Novoselic and Dave Grohl

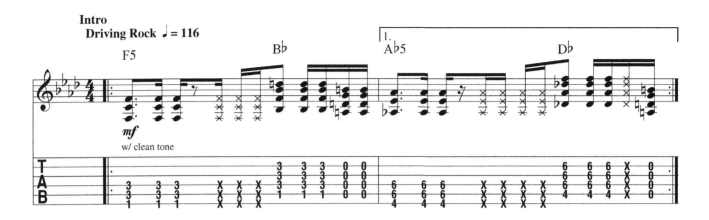

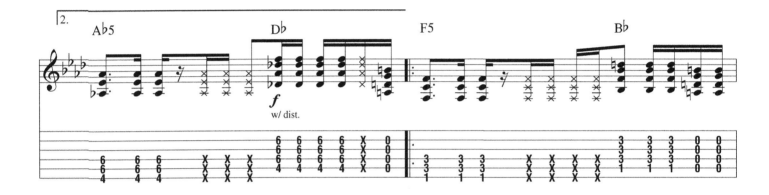

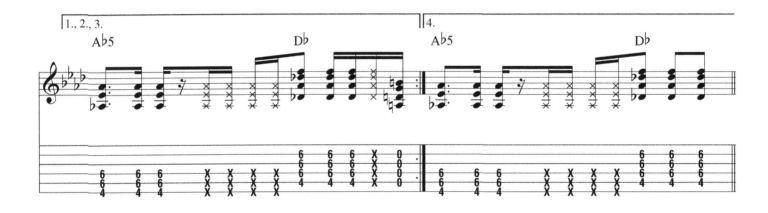

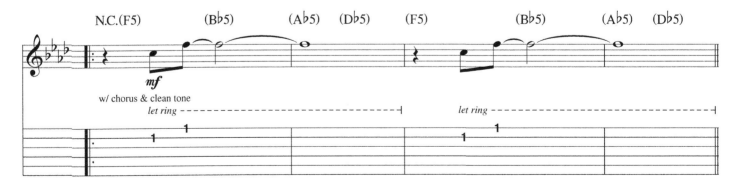

Verse

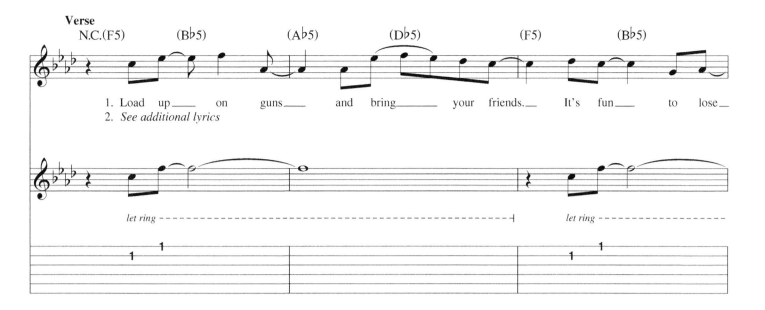

1. Load up____ on guns____ and bring____ your friends.____ It's fun____ to lose____
2. *See additional lyrics*

let ring -   *let ring* - - - - - - - - - - - - - - - -

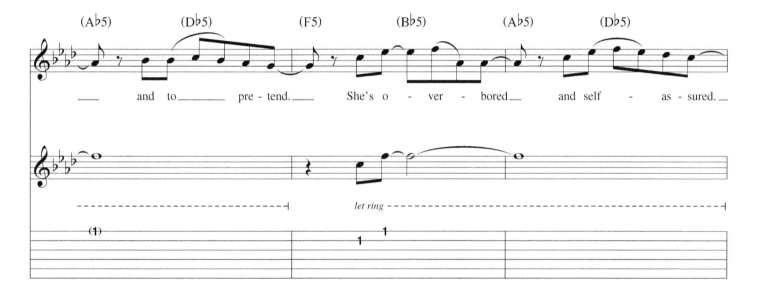

____ and to____ pre - tend.____ She's o - ver - bored____ and self - as - sured.____

let ring - - - - - - - - - - - - - - - -   *let ring* -

Pre-Chorus

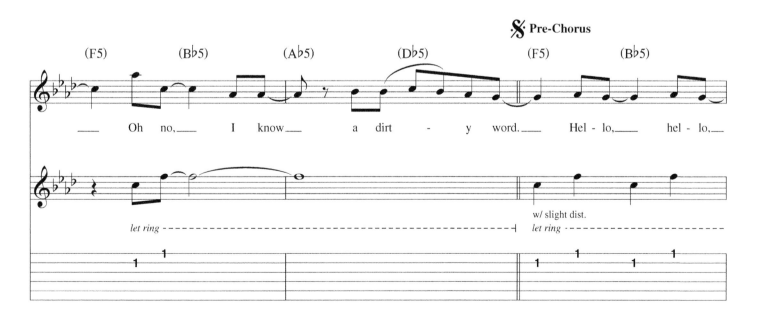

____ Oh no,____ I know____ a dirt - y word.____ Hel - lo,____ hel - lo,____

let ring -   *let ring* - - - - - - - - - - - - - -

w/ slight dist.

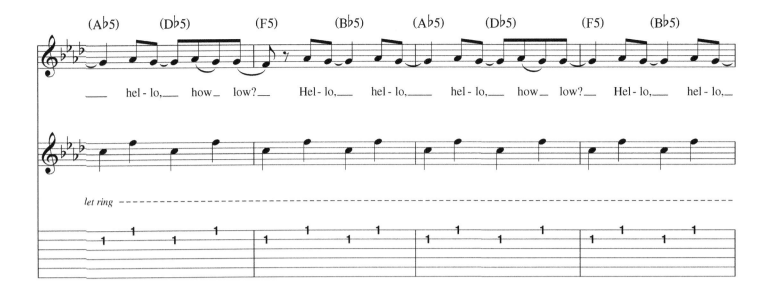

(A♭5)   (D♭5)   (F5)   (B♭5)   (A♭5)   (D♭5)   (F5)   (B♭5)

hel - lo,___ how_ low?___ Hel - lo,___ hel - lo,___ hel - lo,___ how_ low?___ Hel - lo,___ hel - lo,___

let ring

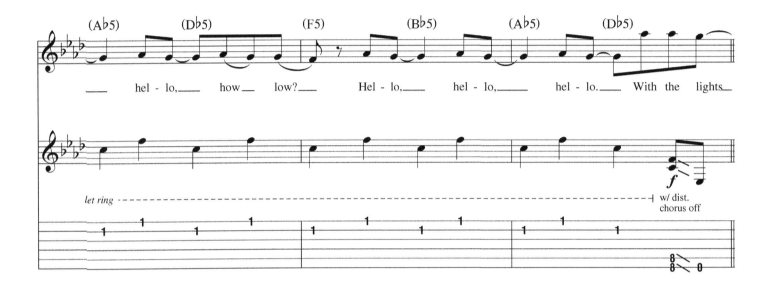

(A♭5)   (D♭5)   (F5)   (B♭5)   (A♭5)   (D♭5)

hel - lo,___ how_ low?___ Hel - lo,___ hel - lo,___ hel - lo.___ With the lights___

let ring -   w/ dist.
chorus off

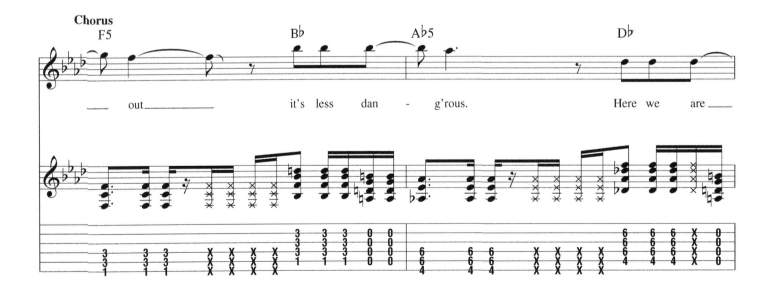

Chorus
F5   B♭   A♭5   D♭

___ out_____ it's less dan - g'rous. Here we are___

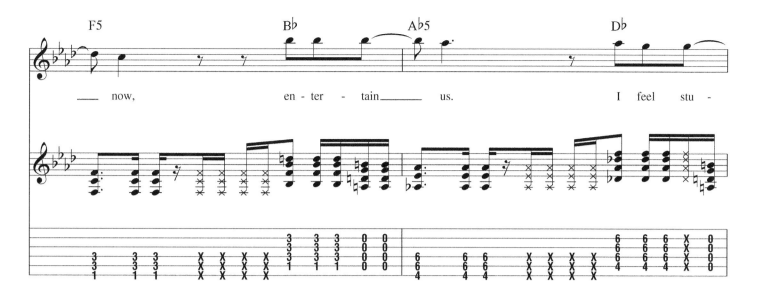

now, en - ter - tain___ us. I feel stu -

- pid___ and con - ta - gious. Here we are___

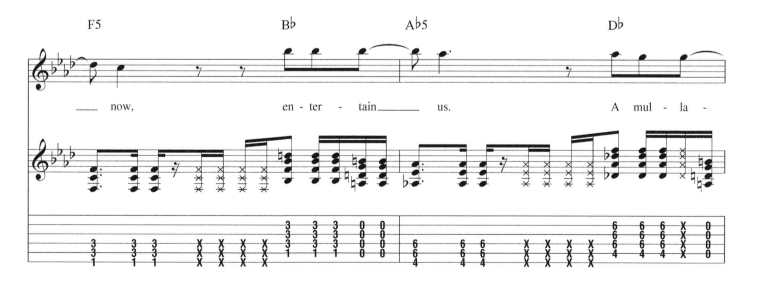

___ now, en - ter - tain___ us. A mul - la -

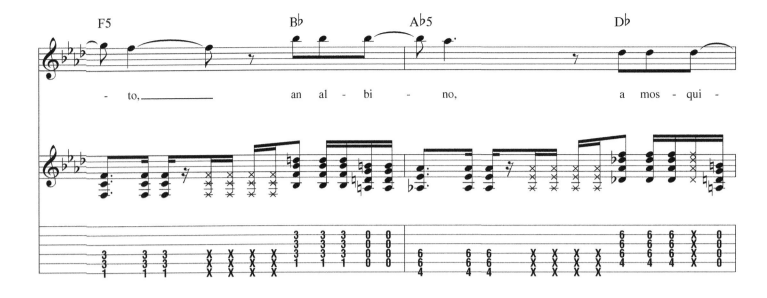

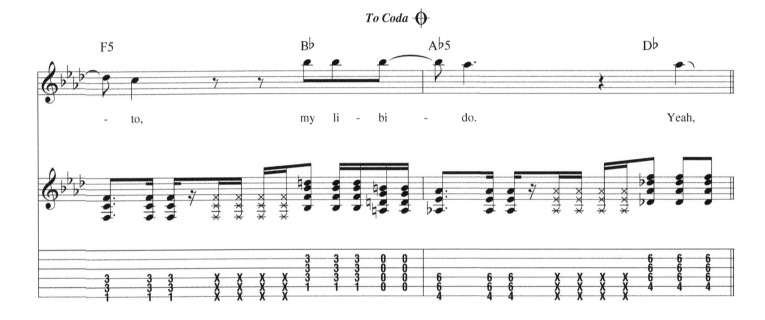

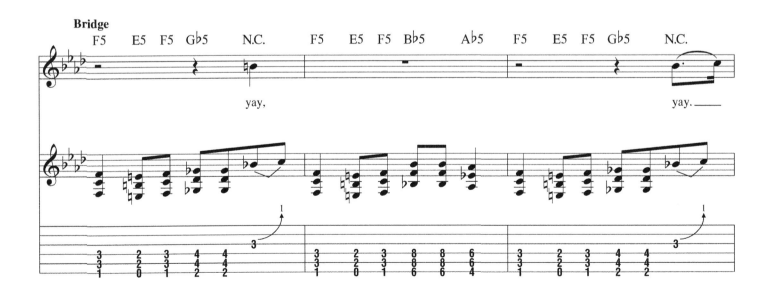

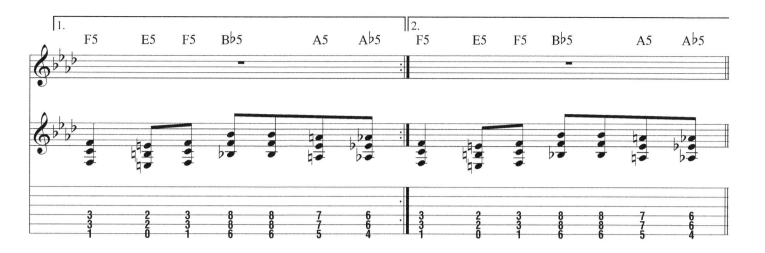

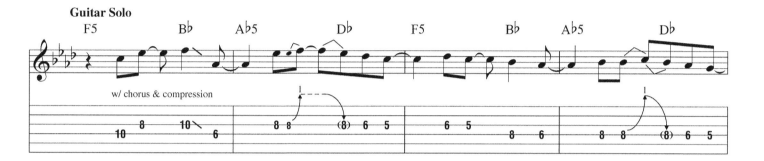

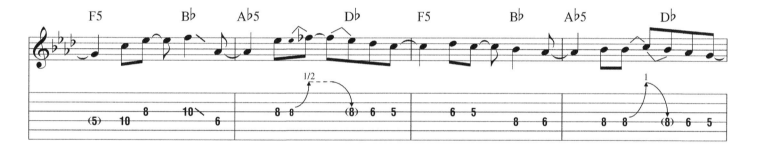

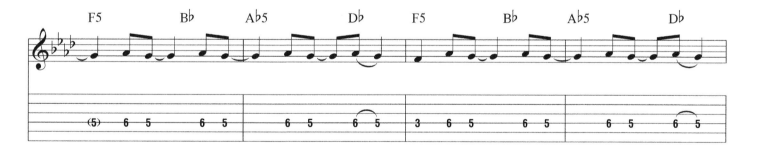

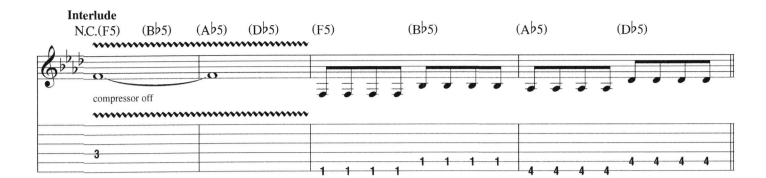

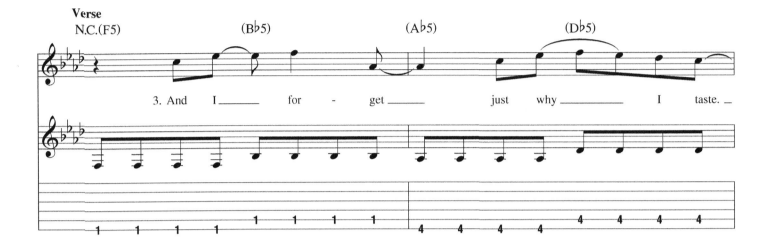

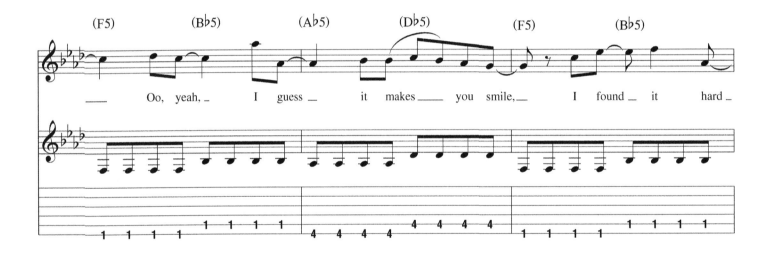

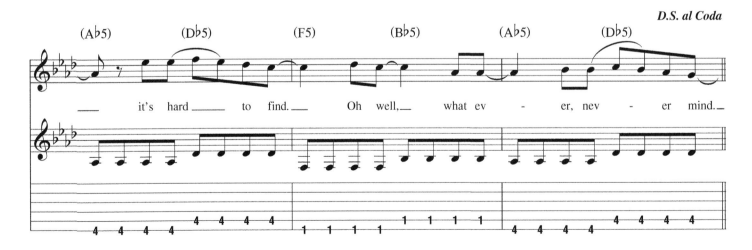

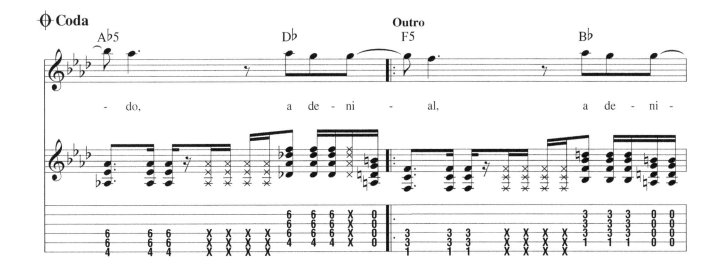

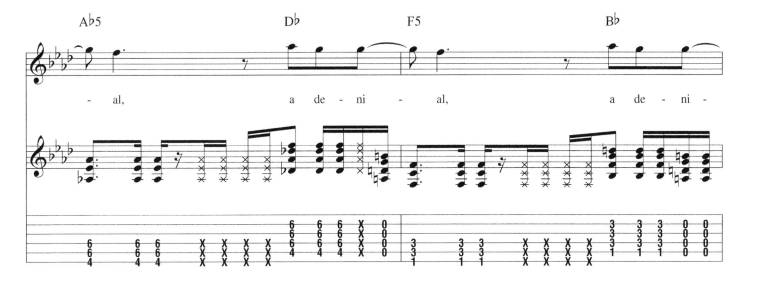

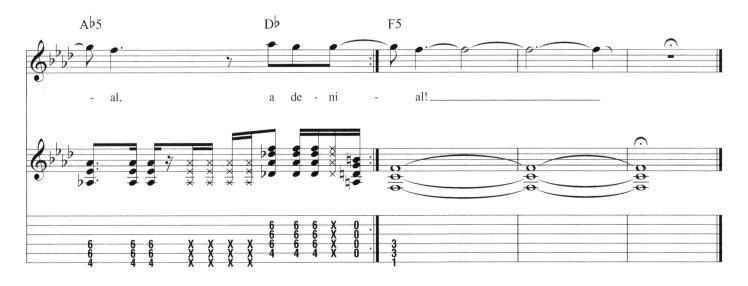

Additional Lyrics

2. I'm worse at what I do best,
   And for this gift I feel blessed.
   Our little group has always been
   And always will until the end.

Summer of '69

Words and Music by Bryan Adams and Jim Vallance

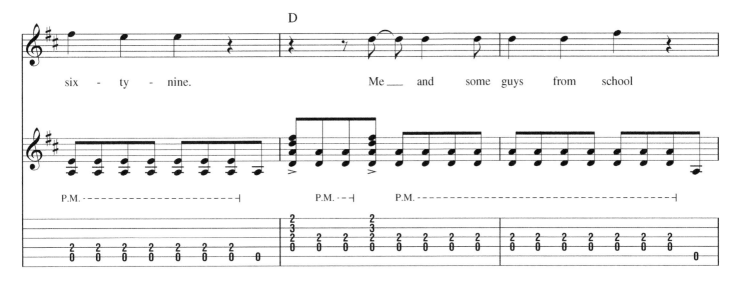

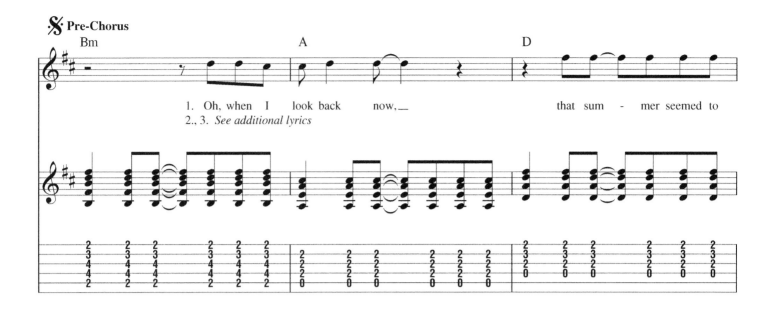

1. Oh, when I look back now,___ that sum - mer seemed to
2., 3. *See additional lyrics*

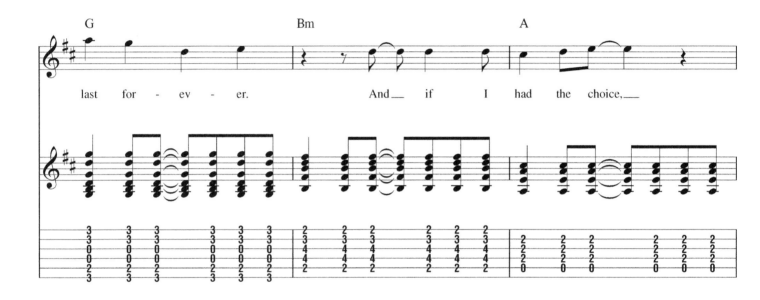

last for - ev - er. And___ if I had the choice,___

yeah,___ I'd al - ways wan - na be there. Those___ were the

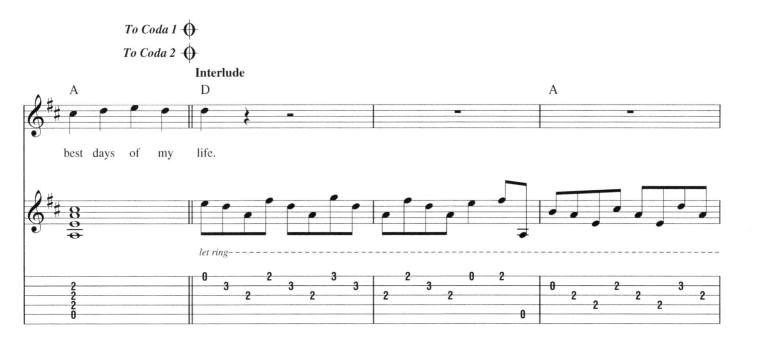

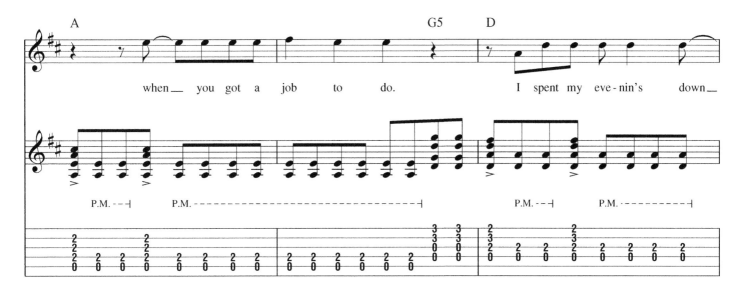

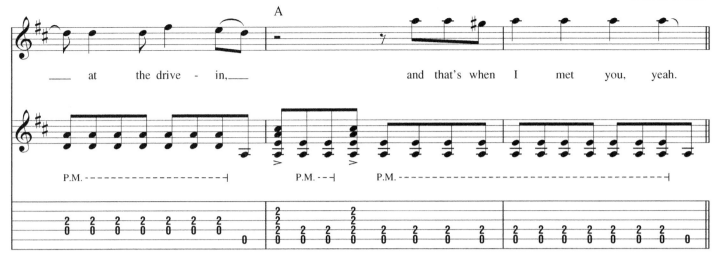

at the drive - in,____ and that's when I met you, yeah.

⊕ Coda 1

Chorus

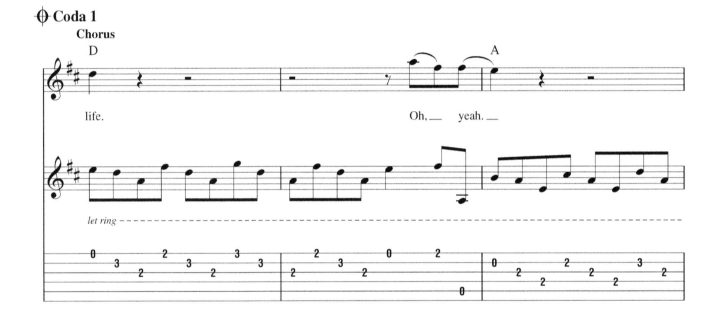

life. Oh,__ yeah.__

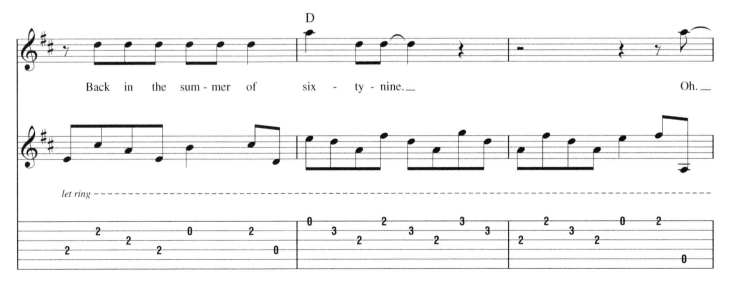

Back in the sum - mer of six - ty - nine.__ Oh.__

Bridge

Man,— we were

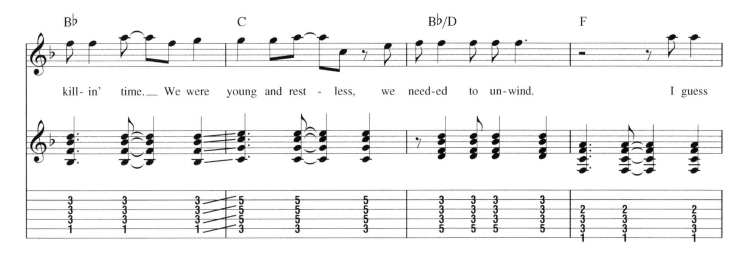

kill-in' time.— We were young and rest-less, we need-ed to un-wind. I guess

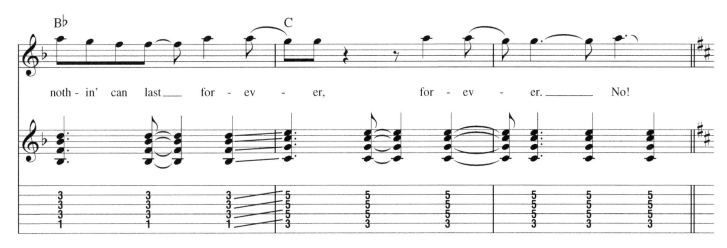

noth-in' can last— for-ev-er, for-ev-er.——— No!

Interlude

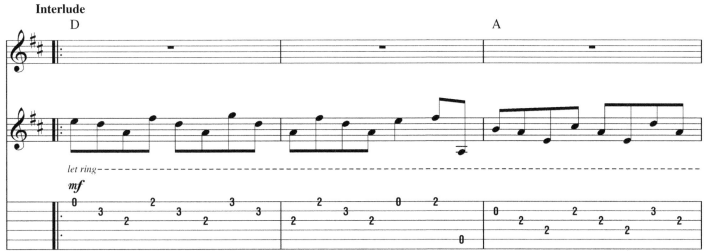

Verse

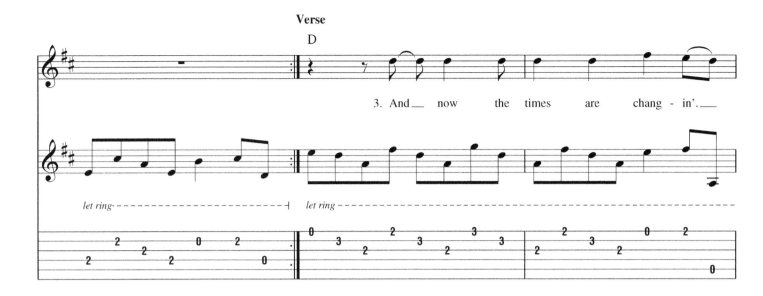

3. And__ now the times are chang - in'.__

Look at ev - 'ry - thing that's come and gone. Some - times__ when I

D.S. al Coda 2

play that old six - string,__ think a - bout ya, won - der what went wrong.

Coda 2

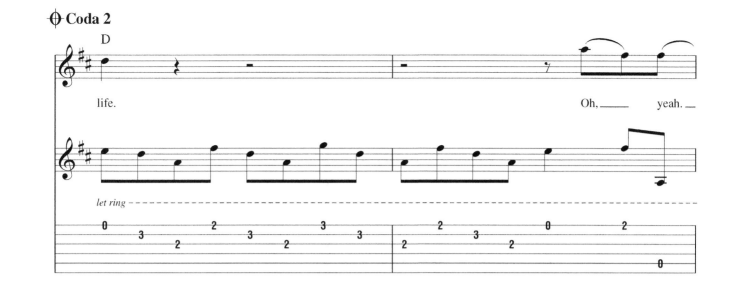

life.   Oh, _____ yeah. _____

Outro

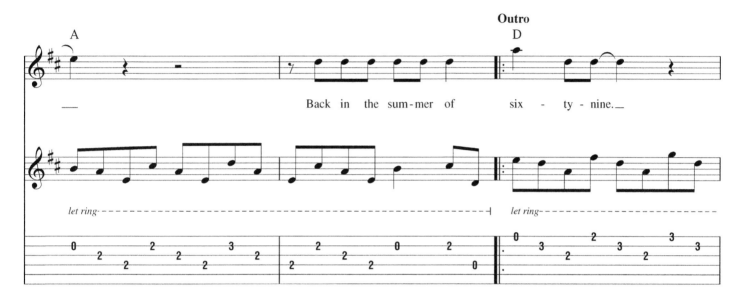

_____   Back in the sum-mer of six - ty - nine. _____

Repeat and fade

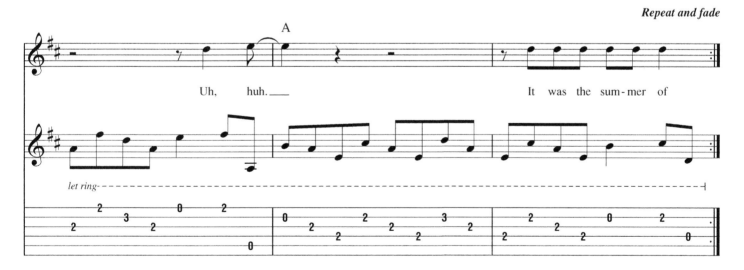

Uh,   huh. _____   It was the sum-mer of

Additional Lyrics

Pre-Chorus 2., 3.   Standin' on your mama's porch

You told me that { you'd wait / it'd last } forever.

Oh, and when you held my hand,
I knew that it was now or never.
Those were the best days of my life.

Sweet Home Chicago

Words and Music by Robert Johnson

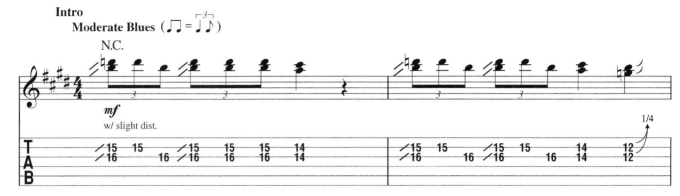

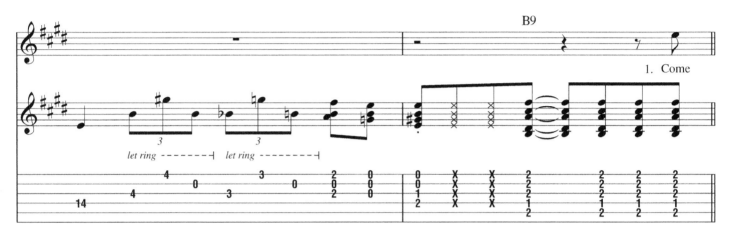

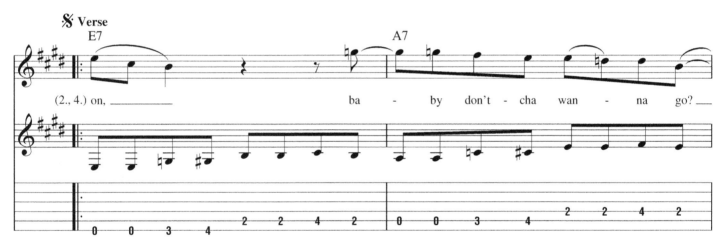

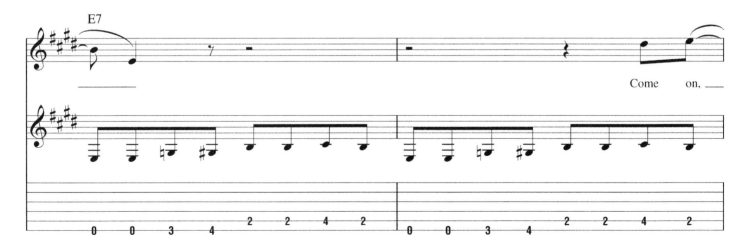

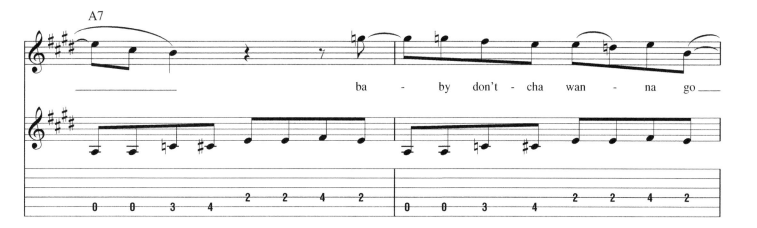

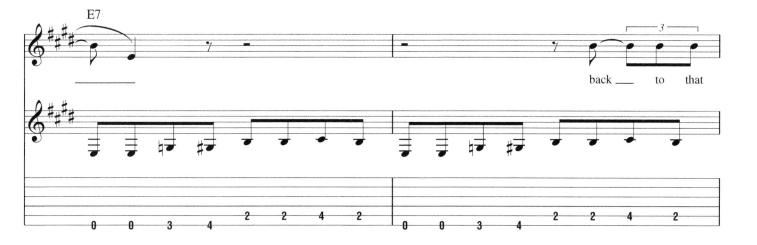

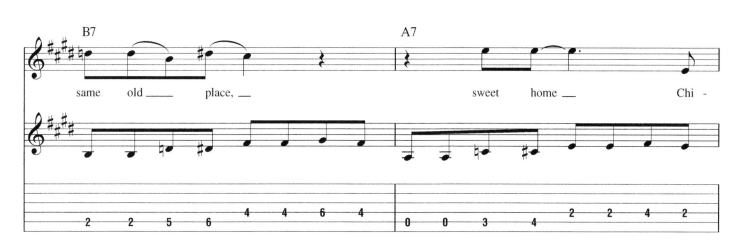

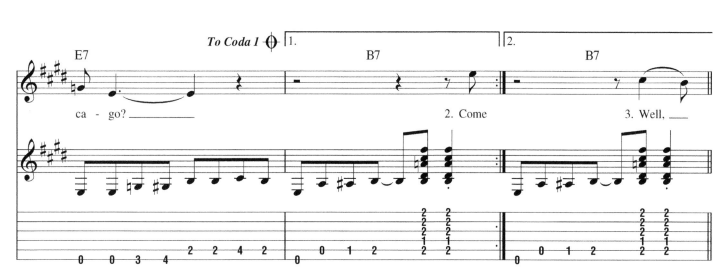

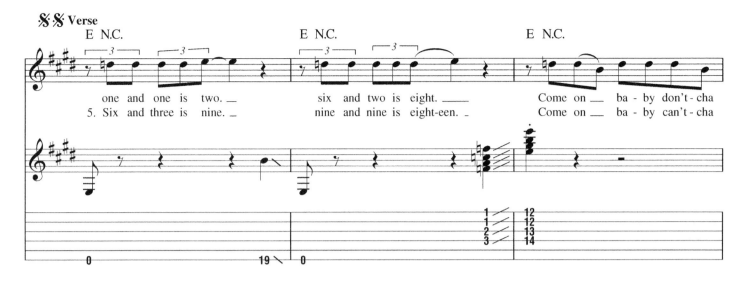

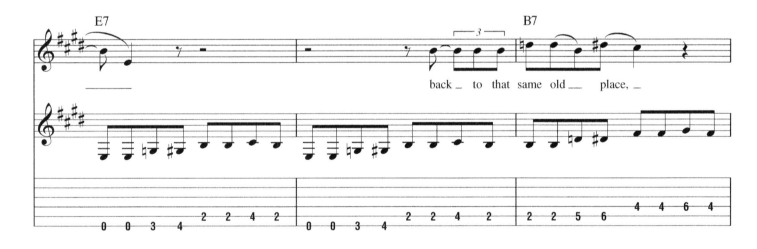

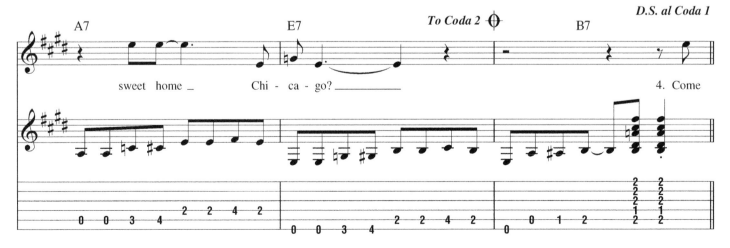

⊕ Coda 1

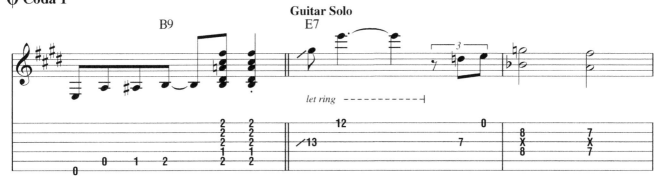

*Hammer from nowhere. (Don't pick.)

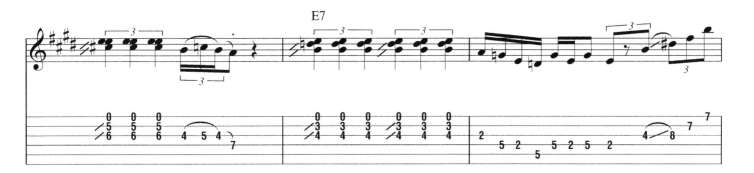

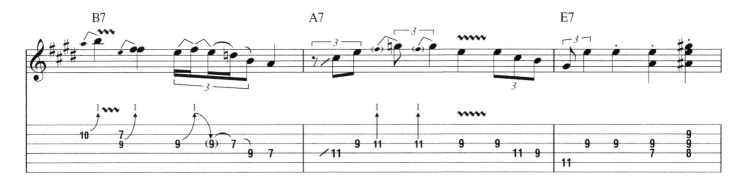

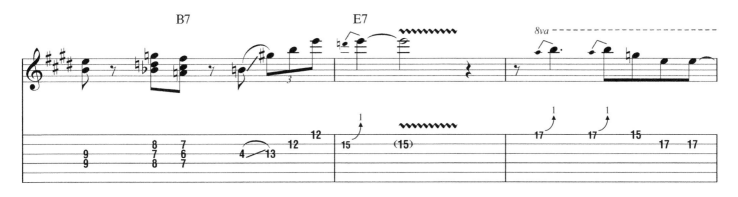

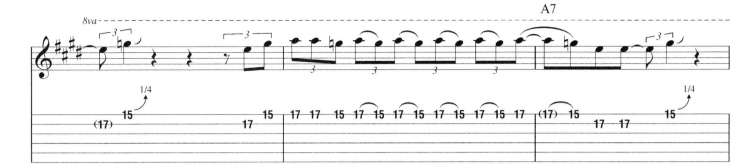

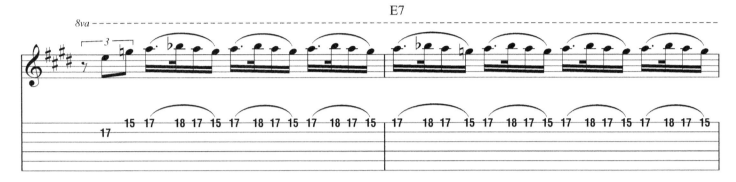

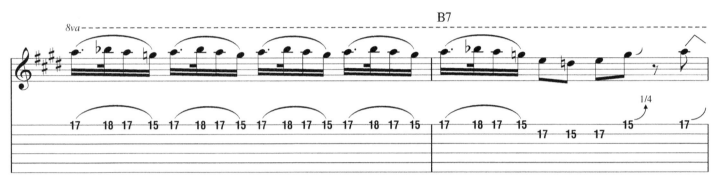

D.S.S. al Coda 2

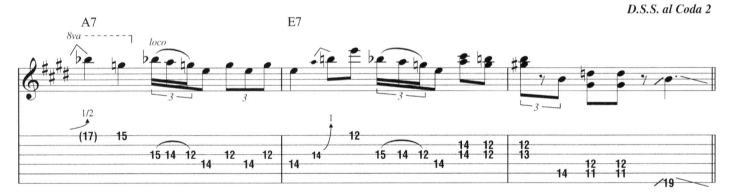

 Coda 2

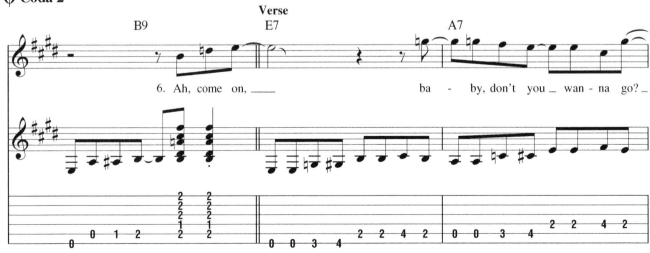

6. Ah, come on, _____ ba - by, don't you _ wan - na go? _

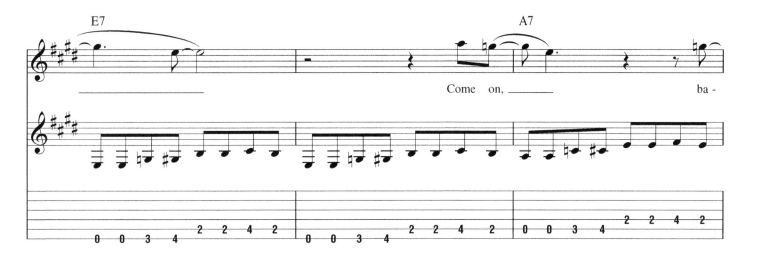

Come on, _____ ba-

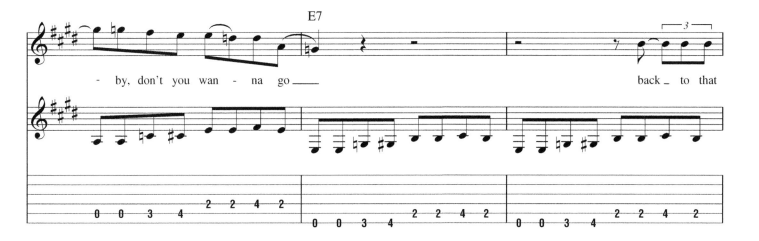

- by, don't you wan - na go _____ back _ to that

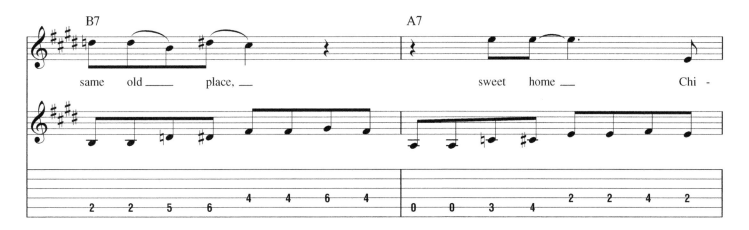

same old _____ place, ___ sweet home ___ Chi -

ca - go? _____

What I Like About You

Words and Music by Michael Skill, Wally Palamarchuk and James Marinos

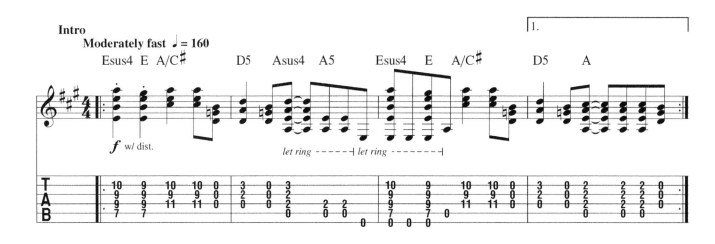

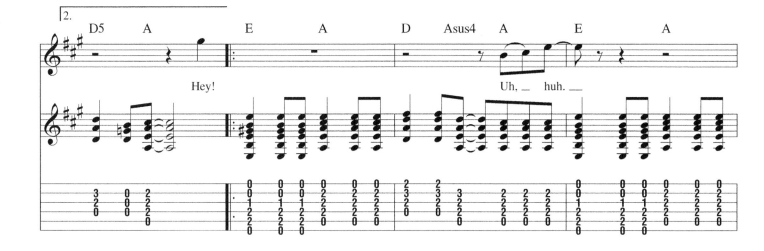

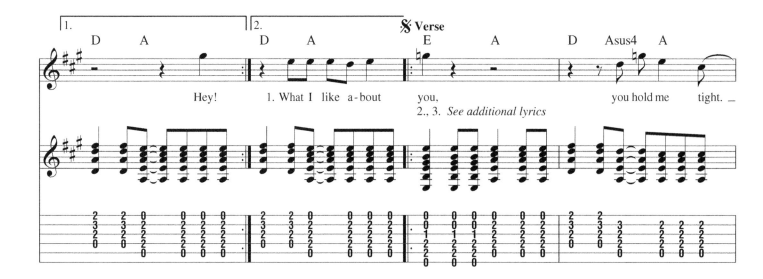

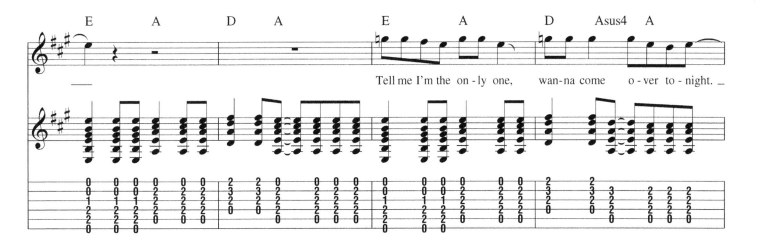

Tell me I'm the on-ly one, wan-na come o-ver to-night. _

Chorus

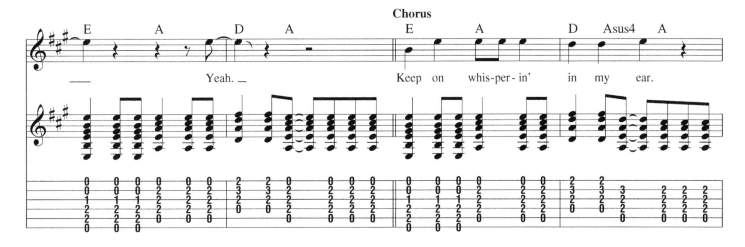

Yeah. _ Keep on whis-per-in' in my ear.

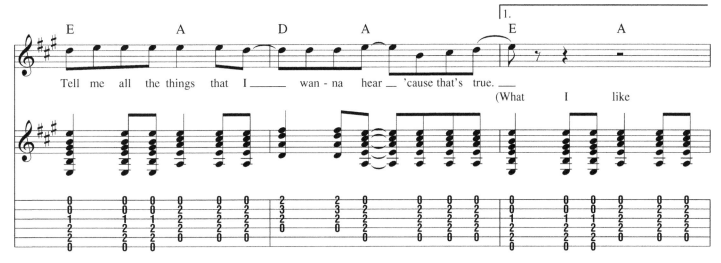

Tell me all the things that I _____ wan-na hear _ 'cause that's true. _
(What I like

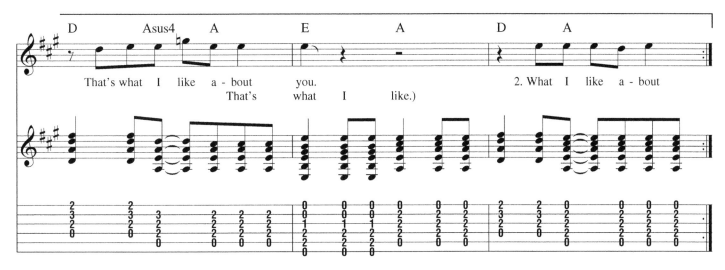

That's what I like a-bout you.
That's what I like.) 2. What I like a-bout

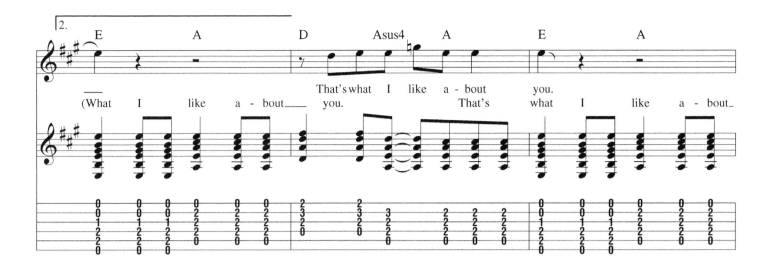

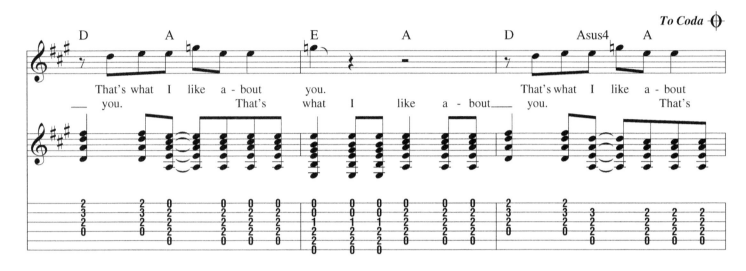

Guitar Solo

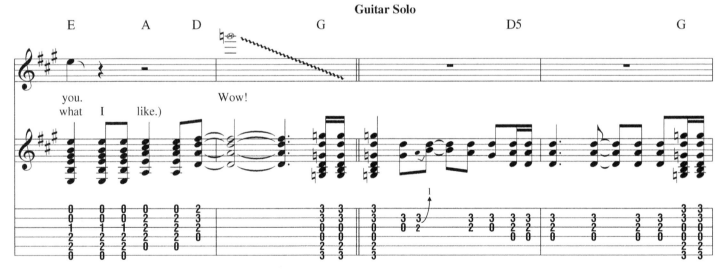

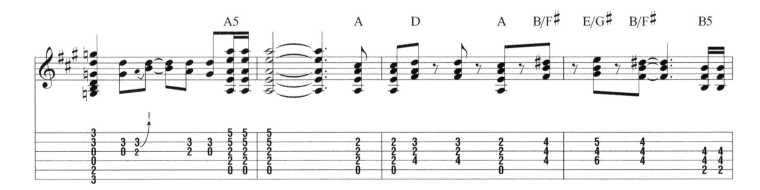

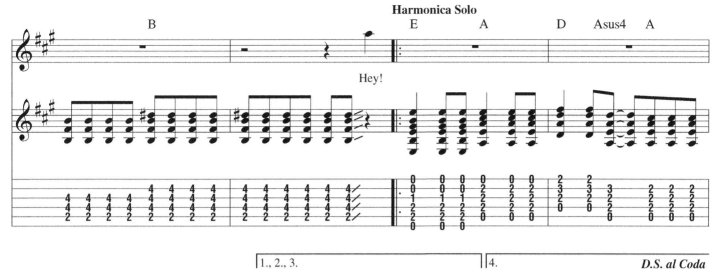

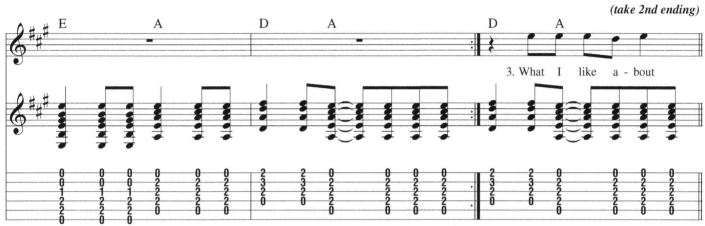

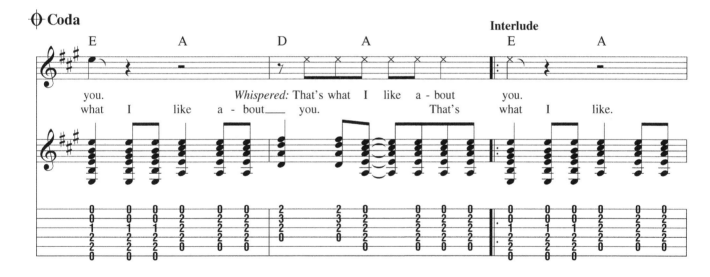

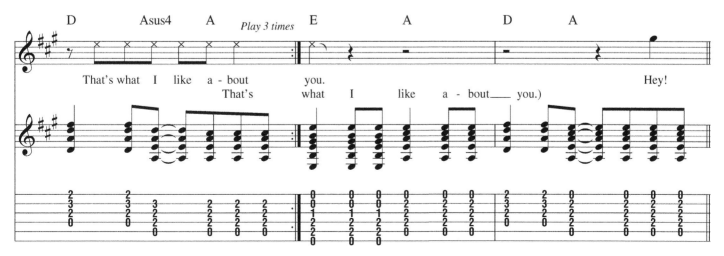

Outro

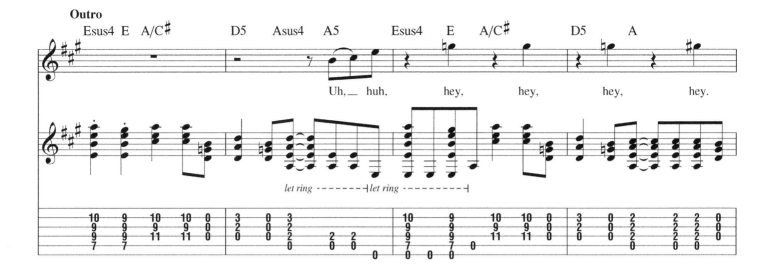

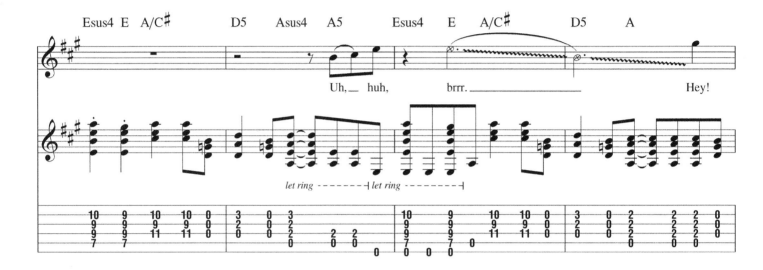

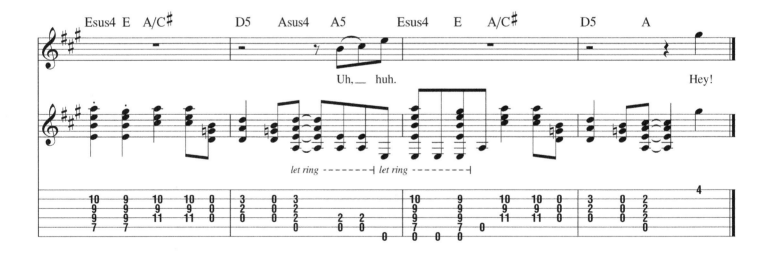

Additional Lyrics

2. What I like about you,
   You really know how to dance.
   When you go uptown jump around,
   Think about true romance. Yeah.

3. What I like about you,
   You keep me warm at night.
   Never wanna let you go,
   Know you make me feel alright. Yeah.

Wonderful Tonight

Words and Music by Eric Clapton

Intro
Moderately slow ♩ = 95
Half-time feel

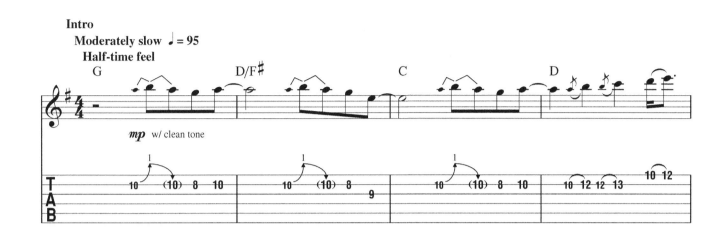

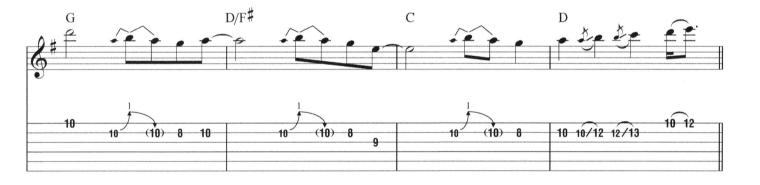

1. It's late in the eve - ning. _____ She's won-d'ring what clothes _
2., 3. *See additional lyrics*

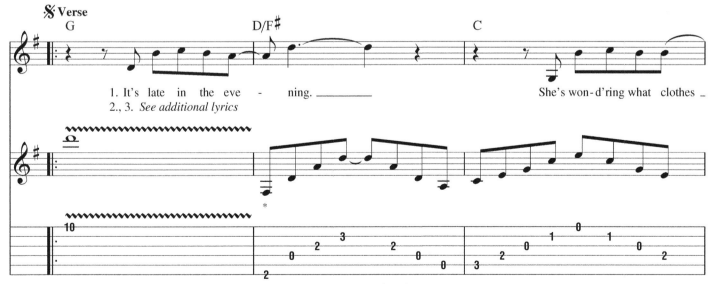

*Let arpeggiated chords ring throughout.

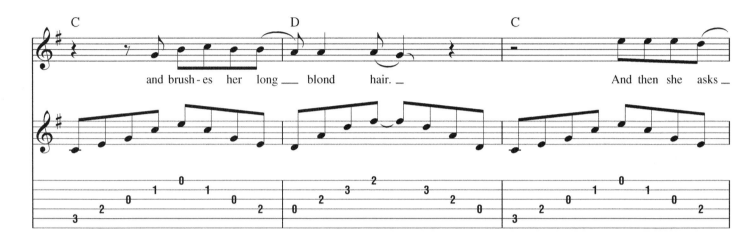

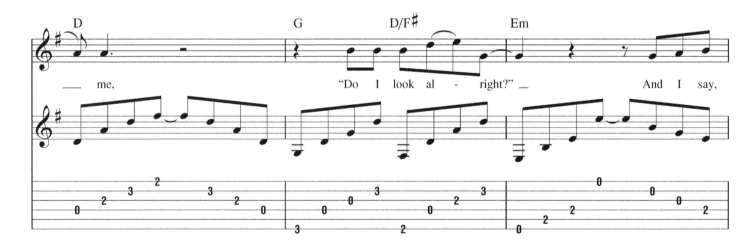

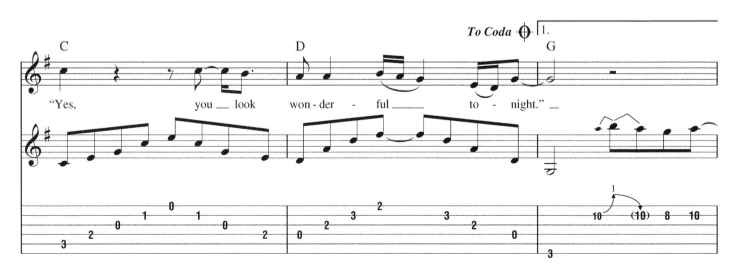

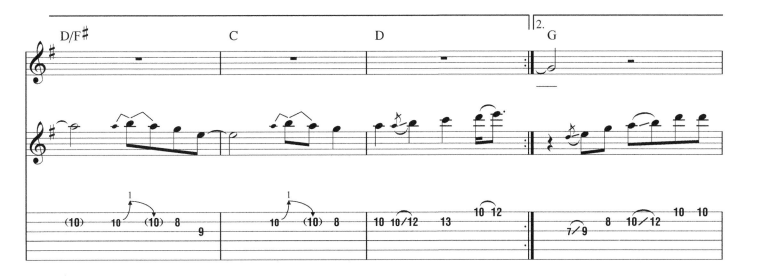

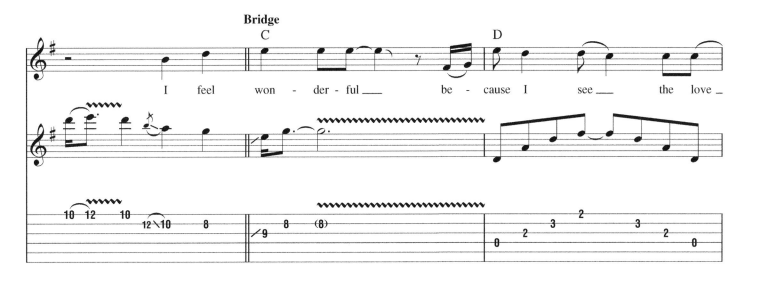

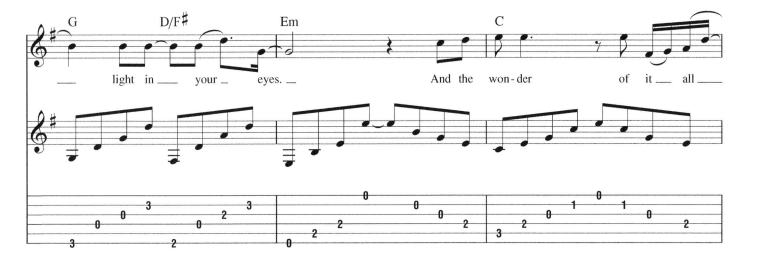

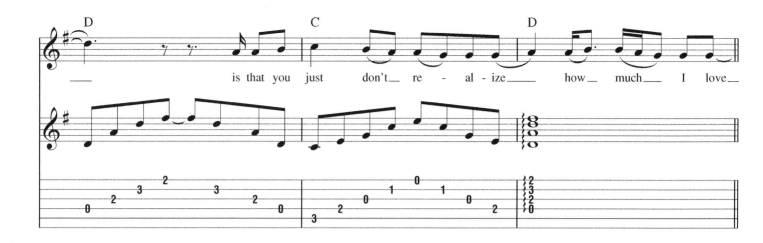

is that you just don't__ re - al - ize__ how__ much__ I love__

Interlude

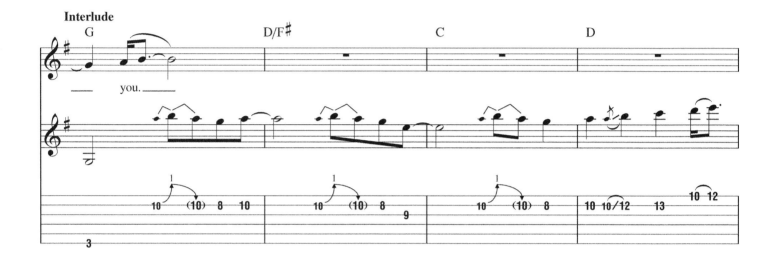

you.____

D.S. al Coda

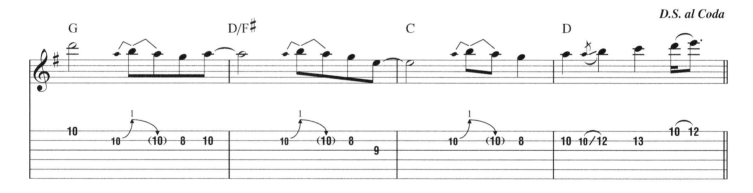

⊕ Coda

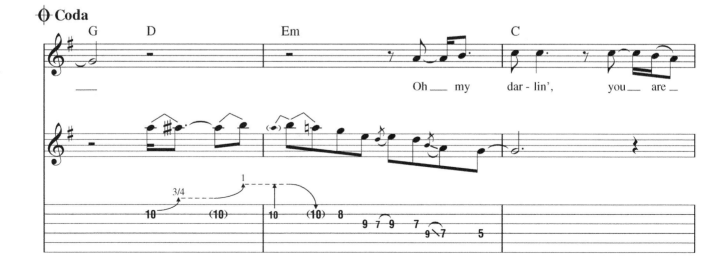

Oh __ my dar - lin', you __ are __

Outro

won - der - ful_____ to - night._____

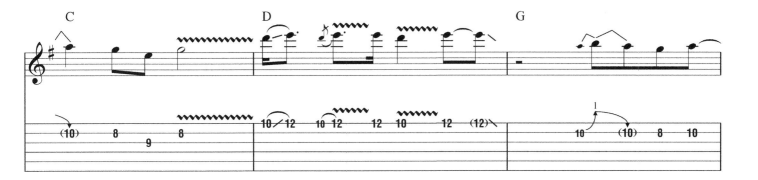

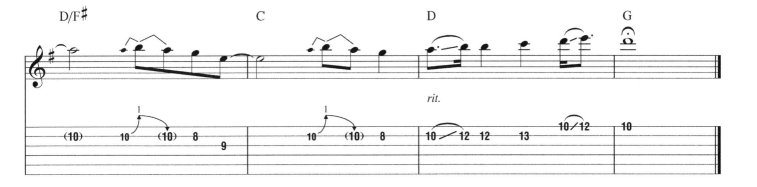

rit.

Additional Lyrics

2. We go to a party, and ev'ryone turns to see
This beautiful lady that's walking around with me.
And then she asks me, "Do you feel alright?"
And I say, "Yes, I feel wonderful tonight."

3. It's time to go home now, and I've got an aching head.
So I give her the car keys and she helps me to bed.
And then I tell her, as I turn out the light,
I say, "My darling, you are wonderful tonight."

Guitar Notation Legend

THE MUSICAL STAFF shows pitches and rhythms and is divided by bar lines into measures. Pitches are named after the first seven letters of the alphabet.

TABLATURE graphically represents the guitar fingerboard. Each horizontal line represents a string, and each number represents a fret.

4th string, 2nd fret   1st & 2nd strings open, played together   open D chord

HALF-STEP BEND: Strike the note and bend up 1/2 step.

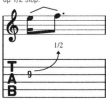

WHOLE-STEP BEND: Strike the note and bend up one step.

GRACE NOTE BEND: Strike the note and bend up as indicated. The first note does not take up any time.

SLIGHT (MICROTONE) BEND: Strike the note and bend up 1/4 step.

BEND AND RELEASE: Strike the note and bend up as indicated, then release back to the original note. Only the first note is struck.

PRE-BEND: Bend the note as indicated, then strike it.

VIBRATO: The string is vibrated by rapidly bending and releasing the note with the fretting hand.

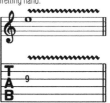

PALM MUTING: The note is partially muted by the pick hand lightly touching the string(s) just before the bridge.

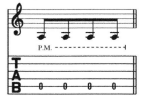

HAMMER-ON: Strike the first (lower) note with one finger, then sound the higher note (on the same string) with another finger by fretting it without picking.

PULL-OFF: Place both fingers on the notes to be sounded. Strike the first note and without picking, pull the finger off to sound the second (lower) note.

LEGATO SLIDE: Strike the first note and then slide the same fret-hand finger up or down to the second note. The second note is not struck.

SHIFT SLIDE: Same as legato slide, except the second note is struck.

TRILL: Very rapidly alternate between the notes indicated by continuously hammering on and pulling off.

TAPPING: Hammer ("tap") the fret indicated with the pick-hand index or middle finger and pull off to the note fretted by the fret hand.

NATURAL HARMONIC: Strike the note while the fret-hand lightly touches the string directly over the fret indicated.

PINCH HARMONIC: The note is fretted normally and a harmonic is produced by adding the edge of the thumb or the tip of the index finger of the pick hand to the normal pick attack.

TREMOLO PICKING: The note is picked as rapidly and continuously as possible.

VIBRATO BAR DIVE AND RETURN: The pitch of the note or chord is dropped a specified number of steps (in rhythm) then returned to the original pitch.

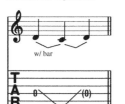

VIBRATO BAR SCOOP: Depress the bar just before striking the note, then quickly release the bar.

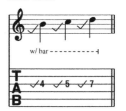

VIBRATO BAR DIP: Strike the note and then immediately drop a specified number of steps, then release back to the original pitch.

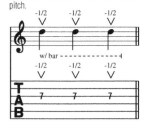

Additional Musical Definitions

(accent)	• Accentuate note (play it louder)	

(staccato) • Play the note short

D.S. al Coda • Go back to the sign (%), then play until the measure marked "***To Coda***", then skip to the section labelled "***Coda***."

D.C. al Fine • Go back to the beginning of the song and play until the measure marked "***Fine***" (end).

Fill • Label used to identify a brief melodic figure which is to be inserted into the arrangement.

N.C. • No Chord

• Repeat measures between signs.

1. 2. • When a repeated section has different endings, play the first ending only the first time and the second ending only the second time.

54

HAL•LEONARD® GUITAR PLAY-ALONG

Complete song lists available online.

This series will help you play your favorite songs quickly and easily. Just follow the tab and listen to the audio to the hear how the guitar should sound, and then play along using the separate backing tracks. Audio files also include software to slow down the tempo without changing pitch. The melody and lyrics are included in the book so that you can sing or simply follow along.

INCLUDES TAB

VOL. 1 – ROCK...00699570 / $17.99
VOL. 2 – ACOUSTIC...................................00699569 / $16.99
VOL. 3 – HARD ROCK...............................00699573 / $17.99
VOL. 4 – POP/ROCK...................................00699571 / $16.99
VOL. 5 – THREE CHORD SONGS.............00300985 / $16.99
VOL. 6 – '90S ROCK...................................00298615 / $16.99
VOL. 7 – BLUES...00699575 / $19.99
VOL. 8 – ROCK...00699585 / $16.99
VOL. 9 – EASY ACOUSTIC SONGS..........00151708 / $16.99
VOL. 10 – ACOUSTIC.................................00699586 / $16.95
VOL. 11 – EARLY ROCK.............................00699579 / $15.99
VOL. 12 – ROCK POP.................................00291724 / $16.99
VOL. 14 – BLUES ROCK.............................00699582 / $16.99
VOL. 15 – R&B..00699583 / $17.99
VOL. 16 – JAZZ...00699584 / $16.99
VOL. 17 – COUNTRY...................................00699588 / $17.99
VOL. 18 – ACOUSTIC ROCK......................00699577 / $15.95
VOL. 20 – ROCKABILLY.............................00699580 / $17.99
VOL. 21 – SANTANA...................................00174525 / $17.99
VOL. 22 – CHRISTMAS...............................00699600 / $15.99
VOL. 23 – SURF..00699635 / $17.99
VOL. 24 – ERIC CLAPTON.........................00699649 / $19.99
VOL. 25 – THE BEATLES...........................00198265 / $19.99
VOL. 26 – ELVIS PRESLEY.........................00699643 / $16.99
VOL. 27 – DAVID LEE ROTH......................00699645 / $16.95
VOL. 28 – GREG KOCH...............................00699646 / $19.99
VOL. 29 – BOB SEGER................................00699647 / $16.99
VOL. 30 – KISS...00699644 / $17.99
VOL. 32 – THE OFFSPRING........................00699653 / $14.95
VOL. 33 – ACOUSTIC CLASSICS...............00699656 / $19.99
VOL. 34 – CLASSIC ROCK..........................00699658 / $17.99
VOL. 35 – HAIR METAL...............................00699660 / $17.99
VOL. 36 – SOUTHERN ROCK.....................00699661 / $19.99
VOL. 37 – ACOUSTIC UNPLUGGED...........00699662 / $22.99
VOL. 38 – BLUES..00699663 / $17.99
VOL. 39 – '80s METAL...............................00699664 / $17.99
VOL. 40 – INCUBUS....................................00699668 / $17.95
VOL. 41 – ERIC CLAPTON..........................00699669 / $17.99
VOL. 42 – COVER BAND HITS....................00211597 / $16.99
VOL. 43 – LYNYRD SKYNYRD....................00699681 / $22.99
VOL. 44 – JAZZ GREATS.............................00699689 / $16.99
VOL. 45 – TV THEMES................................00699718 / $14.95
VOL. 46 – MAINSTREAM ROCK..................00699722 / $16.95
VOL. 47 – JIMI HENDRIX SMASH HITS....00699723 / $19.99
VOL. 48 – AEROSMITH CLASSICS..............00699724 / $17.99
VOL. 49 – STEVIE RAY VAUGHAN.............00699725 / $17.99
VOL. 50 – VAN HALEN: 1978-1984........00110269 / $19.99
VOL. 51 – ALTERNATIVE '90s....................00699727 / $14.99
VOL. 52 – FUNK..00699728 / $15.99
VOL. 53 – DISCO...00699729 / $14.99
VOL. 54 – HEAVY METAL............................00699730 / $17.99
VOL. 55 – POP METAL................................00699731 / $14.95
VOL. 57 – GUNS 'N' ROSES.......................00159922 / $19.99
VOL. 58 – BLINK 182..................................00699772 / $17.99
VOL. 59 – CHET ATKINS.............................00702347 / $17.99
VOL. 60 – 3 DOORS DOWN.......................00699774 / $14.95
VOL. 62 – CHRISTMAS CAROLS................00699798 / $12.95
VOL. 63 – CREEDENCE CLEARWATER
 REVIVAL.................................00699802 / $17.99
VOL. 64 – ULTIMATE OZZY OSBOURNE...00699803 / $19.99
VOL. 66 – THE ROLLING STONES.............00699807 / $19.99
VOL. 67 – BLACK SABBATH.......................00699808 / $17.99
VOL. 68 – PINK FLOYD –
 DARK SIDE OF THE MOON...00699809 / $17.99
VOL. 71 – CHRISTIAN ROCK......................00699824 / $14.95

VOL. 73 – BLUESY ROCK...........................00699829 / $17.99
VOL. 74 – SIMPLE STRUMMING SONGS..00151706 / $19.99
VOL. 75 – TOM PETTY................................00699882 / $19.99
VOL. 76 – COUNTRY HITS.........................00699884 / $16.99
VOL. 77 – BLUEGRASS...............................00699910 / $17.99
VOL. 78 – NIRVANA....................................00700132 / $17.99
VOL. 79 – NEIL YOUNG..............................00700133 / $24.99
VOL. 81 – ROCK ANTHOLOGY..................00700176 / $22.99
VOL. 82 – EASY ROCK SONGS..................00700177 / $17.99
VOL. 84 – STEELY DAN..............................00700200 / $19.99
VOL. 85 – THE POLICE...............................00700269 / $16.99
VOL. 86 – BOSTON......................................00700465 / $19.99
VOL. 87 – ACOUSTIC WOMEN..................00700763 / $14.99
VOL. 88 – GRUNGE.....................................00700467 / $16.99
VOL. 89 – REGGAE.....................................00700468 / $15.99
VOL. 90 – CLASSICAL POP.........................00700469 / $14.99
VOL. 91 – BLUES INSTRUMENTALS.......00700505 / $19.99
VOL. 92 – EARLY ROCK
 INSTRUMENTALS.................00700506 / $17.99
VOL. 93 – ROCK INSTRUMENTALS.........00700507 / $17.99
VOL. 94 – SLOW BLUES.............................00700508 / $16.99
VOL. 95 – BLUES CLASSICS.......................00700509 / $15.99
VOL. 96 – BEST COUNTRY HITS.............00211615 / $16.99
VOL. 97 – CHRISTMAS CLASSICS............00236542 / $14.99
VOL. 99 – ZZ TOP......................................00700762 / $16.99
VOL. 100 – B.B. KING.................................00700466 / $16.99
VOL. 101 – SONGS FOR BEGINNERS......00701917 / $14.99
VOL. 102 – CLASSIC PUNK.......................00700769 / $14.99
VOL. 104 – DUANE ALLMAN.....................00700846 / $22.99
VOL. 105 – LATIN.......................................00700939 / $16.99
VOL. 106 – WEEZER...................................00700958 / $17.99
VOL. 107 – CREAM.....................................00701069 / $17.99
VOL. 108 – THE WHO.................................00701053 / $17.99
VOL. 109 – STEVE MILLER.........................00701054 / $19.99
VOL. 110 – SLIDE GUITAR HITS...............00701055 / $17.99
VOL. 111 – JOHN MELLENCAMP...............00701056 / $14.99
VOL. 112 – QUEEN.....................................00701052 / $16.99
VOL. 113 – JIM CROCE..............................00701058 / $19.99
VOL. 114 – BON JOVI.................................00701060 / $17.99
VOL. 115 – JOHNNY CASH.........................00701070 / $17.99
VOL. 116 – THE VENTURES.......................00701124 / $17.99
VOL. 117 – BRAD PAISLEY.........................00701224 / $16.99
VOL. 118 – ERIC JOHNSON.......................00701353 / $17.99
VOL. 119 – AC/DC CLASSICS.....................00701356 / $19.99
VOL. 120 – PROGRESSIVE ROCK..............00701457 / $14.99
VOL. 121 – U2...00701508 / $17.99
VOL. 122 – CROSBY, STILLS & NASH....00701610 / $16.99
VOL. 123 – LENNON & McCARTNEY
 ACOUSTIC............................00701614 / $16.99
VOL. 124 – SMOOTH JAZZ........................00200664 / $16.99
VOL. 125 – JEFF BECK................................00701687 / $19.99
VOL. 126 – BOB MARLEY...........................00701701 / $17.99
VOL. 127 – 1970s ROCK...........................00701739 / $17.99
VOL. 128 – 1960s ROCK...........................00701740 / $14.99
VOL. 129 – MEGADETH..............................00701741 / $17.99
VOL. 130 – IRON MAIDEN..........................00701742 / $17.99
VOL. 131 – 1990s ROCK...........................00701743 / $14.99
VOL. 132 – COUNTRY ROCK......................00701757 / $15.99
VOL. 133 – TAYLOR SWIFT........................00701894 / $16.99
VOL. 135 – MINOR BLUES.........................00151350 / $17.99
VOL. 136 – GUITAR THEMES....................00701922 / $14.99
VOL. 137 – IRISH TUNES...........................00701966 / $15.99
VOL. 138 – BLUEGRASS CLASSICS..........00701967 / $17.99

VOL. 139 – GARY MOORE...........................00702370 / $17.99
VOL. 140 – MORE STEVIE RAY VAUGHAN.00702396 / $19.99
VOL. 141 – ACOUSTIC HITS........................00702401 / $16.99
VOL. 142 – GEORGE HARRISON................00237697 / $17.99
VOL. 143 – SLASH.......................................00702425 / $19.99
VOL. 144 – DJANGO REINHARDT...............00702531 / $17.99
VOL. 145 – DEF LEPPARD..........................00702532 / $19.99
VOL. 146 – ROBERT JOHNSON..................00702533 / $16.99
VOL. 147 – SIMON & GARFUNKEL............14041591 / $17.99
VOL. 148 – BOB DYLAN..............................14041592 / $17.99
VOL. 149 – AC/DC HITS..............................14041593 / $19.99
VOL. 150 – ZAKK WYLDE............................02501717 / $19.99
VOL. 151 – J.S. BACH.................................02501730 / $16.99
VOL. 152 – JOE BONAMASSA....................02501751 / $24.99
VOL. 153 – RED HOT CHILI PEPPERS....00702990 / $22.99
VOL. 155 – ERIC CLAPTON UNPLUGGED.00703085 / $17.99
VOL. 156 – SLAYER.....................................00703770 / $19.99
VOL. 157 – FLEETWOOD MAC....................00101382 / $17.99
VOL. 159 – WES MONTGOMERY...............00102593 / $22.99
VOL. 160 – T-BONE WALKER.....................00102641/ $17.99
VOL. 161 – THE EAGLES ACOUSTIC........00102659 / $19.99
VOL. 162 – THE EAGLES HITS....................00102667 / $17.99
VOL. 163 – PANTERA..................................00103036 / $19.99
VOL. 164 – VAN HALEN: 1986-1995.....00110270 / $19.99
VOL. 165 – GREEN DAY...............................00210343 / $17.99
VOL. 166 – MODERN BLUES.......................00700764 / $16.99
VOL. 167 – DREAM THEATER......................00111938 / $24.99
VOL. 168 – KISS...00113421 / $17.99
VOL. 169 – TAYLOR SWIFT........................00115982 / $16.99
VOL. 170 – THREE DAYS GRACE...............00117337 / $16.99
VOL. 171 – JAMES BROWN.........................00117420 / $16.99
VOL. 172 – THE DOOBIE BROTHERS.....00119670 / $17.99
VOL. 173 – TRANS-SIBERIAN
 ORCHESTRA.........................00119907 / $19.99
VOL. 174 – SCORPIONS.............................00122119 / $19.99
VOL. 175 – MICHAEL SCHENKER............00122127 / $17.99
VOL. 176 – BLUES BREAKERS WITH JOHN
 MAYALL & ERIC CLAPTON.......00122132 / $19.99
VOL. 177 – ALBERT KING...........................00123271 / $17.99
VOL. 178 – JASON MRAZ.............................00124165 / $17.99
VOL. 179 – RAMONES.................................00127073 / $16.99
VOL. 180 – BRUNO MARS............................00129706 / $16.99
VOL. 181 – JACK JOHNSON.......................00129854 / $16.99
VOL. 182 – SOUNDGARDEN.......................00138161 / $17.99
VOL. 183 – BUDDY GUY..............................00138240 / $17.99
VOL. 184 – KENNY WAYNE SHEPHERD...00138258 / $17.99
VOL. 185 – JOE SATRIANI...........................00139457 / $19.99
VOL. 186 – GRATEFUL DEAD......................00139459 / $17.99
VOL. 187 – JOHN DENVER...........................00140839 / $19.99
VOL. 188 – MÖTLEY CRÜE...........................00141145 / $19.99
VOL. 189 – JOHN MAYER.............................00144350 / $19.99
VOL. 190 – DEEP PURPLE............................00146152 / $19.99
VOL. 191 – PINK FLOYD CLASSICS.........00146164 / $17.99
VOL. 192 – JUDAS PRIEST...........................00151352 / $19.99
VOL. 193 – STEVE VAI.................................00156028 / $19.99
VOL. 194 – PEARL JAM................................00157925 / $17.99
VOL. 195 – METALLICA: 1983-1988.......00234291 / $22.99
VOL. 196 – METALLICA: 1991-2016.......00234292 / $19.99

Prices, contents, and availability subject to change without notice.

HAL•LEONARD®
www.halleonard.com

EASY GUITAR WITH NOTES & TAB

This series features simplified arrangements with notes, tab, chord charts, and strum and pick patterns.

MIXED FOLIOS

00702287	Acoustic	$19.99
00702002	Acoustic Rock Hits for Easy Guitar	$15.99
00702166	All-Time Best Guitar Collection	$19.99
00702232	Best Acoustic Songs for Easy Guitar	$16.99
00119835	Best Children's Songs	$16.99
00703055	The Big Book of Nursery Rhymes & Children's Songs	$16.99
00698978	Big Christmas Collection	$19.99
00702394	Bluegrass Songs for Easy Guitar	$15.99
00289632	Bohemian Rhapsody	$19.99
00703387	Celtic Classics	$14.99
00224808	Chart Hits of 2016-2017	$14.99
00267383	Chart Hits of 2017-2018	$14.99
00334293	Chart Hits of 2019-2020	$16.99
00702149	Children's Christian Songbook	$9.99
00702028	Christmas Classics	$8.99
00101779	Christmas Guitar	$14.99
00702141	Classic Rock	$8.95
00159642	Classical Melodies	$12.99
00253933	Disney/Pixar's Coco	$16.99
00702203	CMT's 100 Greatest Country Songs	$34.99
00702283	The Contemporary Christian Collection	$16.99
00196954	Contemporary Disney	$19.99
00702239	Country Classics for Easy Guitar	$24.99

00702257	Easy Acoustic Guitar Songs	$16.99
00702041	Favorite Hymns for Easy Guitar	$12.99
00222701	Folk Pop Songs	$17.99
00126894	Frozen	$14.99
00333922	Frozen 2	$14.99
00702286	Glee	$16.99
00702160	The Great American Country Songbook	$19.99
00702148	Great American Gospel for Guitar	$14.99
00702050	Great Classical Themes for Easy Guitar	$9.99
00275088	The Greatest Showman	$17.99
00148030	Halloween Guitar Songs	$14.99
00702273	Irish Songs	$12.99
00192503	Jazz Classics for Easy Guitar	$16.99
00702275	Jazz Favorites for Easy Guitar	$17.99
00702274	Jazz Standards for Easy Guitar	$19.99
00702162	Jumbo Easy Guitar Songbook	$24.99
00232285	La La Land	$16.99
00702258	Legends of Rock	$14.99
00702189	MTV's 100 Greatest Pop Songs	$34.99
00702272	1950s Rock	$16.99
00702271	1960s Rock	$16.99
00702270	1970s Rock	$19.99
00702269	1980s Rock	$15.99
00702268	1990s Rock	$19.99
00369043	Rock Songs for Kids	$14.99

00109725	Once	$14.99
00702187	Selections from O Brother Where Art Thou?	$19.99
00702178	100 Songs for Kids	$14.99
00702515	Pirates of the Caribbean	$17.99
00702125	Praise and Worship for Guitar	$14.99
00287930	Songs from *A Star Is Born, The Greatest Showman, La La Land*, and More Movie Musicals	$16.99
00702285	Southern Rock Hits	$12.99
00156420	Star Wars Music	$16.99
00121535	30 Easy Celtic Guitar Solos	$16.99
00702156	3-Chord Rock	$12.99
00244654	Top Hits of 2017	$14.99
00283786	Top Hits of 2018	$14.99
00702294	Top Worship Hits	$17.99
00702255	VH1's 100 Greatest Hard Rock Songs	$34.99
00702175	VH1's 100 Greatest Songs of Rock and Roll	$29.99
00702253	Wicked	$12.99

ARTIST COLLECTIONS

00702267	AC/DC for Easy Guitar	$16.99
00702598	Adele for Easy Guitar	$15.99
00156221	Adele – 25	$16.99
00702040	Best of the Allman Brothers	$16.99
00702865	J.S. Bach for Easy Guitar	$15.99
00702169	Best of The Beach Boys	$15.99
00702292	The Beatles — 1	$22.99
00125796	Best of Chuck Berry	$15.99
00702201	The Essential Black Sabbath	$15.99
00702250	blink-182 — Greatest Hits	$17.99
02501615	Zac Brown Band — The Foundation	$17.99
02501621	Zac Brown Band — You Get What You Give	$16.99
00702043	Best of Johnny Cash	$17.99
00702090	Eric Clapton's Best	$16.99
00702086	Eric Clapton — from the Album Unplugged	$17.99
00702202	The Essential Eric Clapton	$17.99
00702053	Best of Patsy Cline	$15.99
00222697	Very Best of Coldplay – 2nd Edition	$16.99
00702229	The Very Best of Creedence Clearwater Revival	$16.99
00702145	Best of Jim Croce	$16.99
00702278	Crosby, Stills & Nash	$12.99
14042809	Bob Dylan	$15.99
00702276	Fleetwood Mac — Easy Guitar Collection	$17.99
00139462	The Very Best of Grateful Dead	$16.99
00702136	Best of Merle Haggard	$16.99
00702227	Jimi Hendrix — Smash Hits	$19.99
00702288	Best of Hillsong United	$12.99
00702236	Best of Antonio Carlos Jobim	$15.99
00702245	Elton John — Greatest Hits 1970–2002	$19.99

00129855	Jack Johnson	$16.99
00702204	Robert Johnson	$14.99
00702234	Selections from Toby Keith — 35 Biggest Hits	$12.95
00702003	Kiss	$16.99
00702216	Lynyrd Skynyrd	$16.99
00702182	The Essential Bob Marley	$16.99
00146081	Maroon 5	$14.99
00121925	Bruno Mars – Unorthodox Jukebox	$12.99
00702248	Paul McCartney — All the Best	$14.99
00125484	The Best of MercyMe	$12.99
00702209	Steve Miller Band — Young Hearts (Greatest Hits)	$12.95
00124167	Jason Mraz	$15.99
00702096	Best of Nirvana	$16.99
00702211	The Offspring — Greatest Hits	$17.99
00138026	One Direction	$17.99
00702030	Best of Roy Orbison	$17.99
00702144	Best of Ozzy Osbourne	$14.99
00702279	Tom Petty	$17.99
00102911	Pink Floyd	$17.99
00702139	Elvis Country Favorites	$19.99
00702293	The Very Best of Prince	$19.99
00699415	Best of Queen for Guitar	$16.99
00109279	Best of R.E.M.	$14.99
00702208	Red Hot Chili Peppers — Greatest Hits	$16.99
00198960	The Rolling Stones	$17.99
00174793	The Very Best of Santana	$16.99
00702196	Best of Bob Seger	$16.99
00146046	Ed Sheeran	$15.99
00702252	Frank Sinatra — Nothing But the Best	$12.99
00702010	Best of Rod Stewart	$17.99
00702049	Best of George Strait	$17.99

00702259	Taylor Swift for Easy Guitar	$15.99
00359800	Taylor Swift – Easy Guitar Anthology	$24.99
00702260	Taylor Swift — Fearless	$14.99
00139727	Taylor Swift — 1989	$17.99
00115960	Taylor Swift — Red	$16.99
00253667	Taylor Swift — Reputation	$17.99
00702290	Taylor Swift — Speak Now	$16.99
00232849	Chris Tomlin Collection – 2nd Edition	$14.99
00702226	Chris Tomlin — See the Morning	$12.95
00148643	Train	$14.99
00702427	U2 — 18 Singles	$19.99
00702108	Best of Stevie Ray Vaughan	$17.99
00279005	The Who	$14.99
00702123	Best of Hank Williams	$15.99
00194548	Best of John Williams	$14.99
00702228	Neil Young — Greatest Hits	$17.99
00119133	Neil Young — Harvest	$14.99

Prices, contents and availability subject to change without notice.

Visit Hal Leonard online at **halleonard.com**

1221

306